Video Interviews with 14 Professionals
Working in Japan

Alice Gordenker / John Rucynski

CENGAGE
Learning

Working in Japan [Text Only]—Video Interviews with 14 Professionals

Alice Gordenker / John Rucynski

© 2015 Cengage Learning K.K.

Photo Credits:
front cover (all), pp. 12, 18, 24, 30, 36, 42, 48, 54, 60, 66, 72, 78, 84, 90: © Tamami Machida/Cengage Learning K.K.; p. 13: (b, c) courtesy of David White; p. 19: (a–c) courtesy of Merve Ozkok; p. 25: (a, c, d) courtesy of Tiziana Alamprese; p. 31: (a, d) courtesy of Alexander O. Smith; p. 37: (b, d) courtesy of Lam Thanh Huyen; p. 43: (a, d) courtesy of Shigeharu Asagiri, (c) © Yoshinari Baba; p. 49: (a–c) courtesy of Andrew Wakatsuki-Robinson; p. 55: (a) courtesy of Astrid Klein, (b) © Koichi Torimura, (d) © Klein Dytham architecture; p. 61: (all) courtesy of Sachiko Takao; p. 67: (all) courtesy of Christopher Faulkner; p. 73: (b, d) courtesy of Annie Chang; p. 79: (a, b) courtesy of Sreekumar Bhanuvikraman Pillai Ambika; p. 85: (all) courtesy of Philippe Batton; p. 91: (b–d) courtesy of Elizabeth Oliver
Unless noted above, all photos are from the *Working in Japan* Video Program: © Cengage Learning K.K.

Acknowledgments:
The publisher would like to thank the following for their cooperation in filming for this textbook:
(In order of units) Taito-ku Film Commission; Meiji Gakuin University; Dr. Paul Hullah (Meiji Gakuin University); H.I.S. Co., Ltd.; Fiat Chrysler Japan; Lawson, Inc.; Coedo Brewery; Shukutoku Elementary School; Klein Dytham architecture; Global Agents Co., Ltd.; WORLD NEIGHBORS Gokokuji; Mitsui & Co., Ltd.; EP Consulting Services Corporation; Le Petit Tonneau; Animal Refuge Kansai

For permission to use material from this textbook or product, e-mail to **eltjapan@cengage.com**

ISBN: 978-4-86312-409-7

Cengage Learning K.K.
No. 2 Funato Building 5th Floor
1-11-11 Kudankita, Chiyoda-ku
Tokyo 102-0073
Japan

Tel: 03-3511-4392
Fax: 03-3511-4391

Preface

....

Your school years are an exciting time of life—a time to explore, discover your interests and learn your strengths. It is also a time to prepare for your working life after graduation. There are a lot of decisions to make: "What do I want to do?" "What sort of working life would I like?" Whatever decisions you make, English is a valuable tool that will open doors for you and make new things possible.

Working in Japan is an opportunity to learn specific English vocabulary and phrases chosen because they will help you in your working life. But it is much more than that. It is also an opportunity to meet 14 interesting people and hear their views on working in Japan. They come from many different countries. They work in many different professions. All of them feel positive about working in Japan. Learn from them, and let their experience guide you, as you plan now for your future working in Japan—and the world!

Alice Gordenker

....

When you study a foreign language, you should also study foreign culture. However, culture does not only mean something which comes from a foreign country. There is also the culture of the workplace. After your school years, you will enter this new culture.

Working in Japan thus offers you the best of both worlds. As you study English by watching the interviews in this book, you can also learn about foreign culture and the culture of work. The people featured in this book come from a wide range of countries and professional backgrounds. Listening to their comments about working in Japan will give you a deeper understanding of both similarities and differences when it comes to work. Additionally, you will sharpen your listening skills by hearing a variety of English accents. Finally, you will also acquire valuable work-related vocabulary.

You don't necessarily need to live outside of Japan to experience multicultural environments. This book will show you that Japan already has a globalized workforce. We made this book as a useful step for you in becoming a part of this exciting new world.

John Rucynski, Jr.

....

Table of Contents

Speaking Practice	Sharing Your Ideas	Reading Passgae
a team player	Being a Good Co-worker	There's More to Life Than Work
recommend	Having Fun While Traveling	Japan Needs Muslim-Friendly Meals
What's your secret?	Staying Positive	Money Isn't Everything
explore different interests	Learning Foreign Languages	Why Learn Japanese?
the rest of	What Do You Love About Japan?	*Kisetsukan*: "Sense of the Seasons" as a Marketing Tool
pay off	Making Your English Understood	Think Global, Act Local
bring out the best in	Teaching English to Children	Trouble for "Tall Poppies"

Speaking Practice	Sharing Your Ideas	Reading Passgae
open to new things	Finding the Best Job	Finally! A Better Way to Make Presentations!
on top of that	Exploring Japan	Internships —A Win-Win Situation
follow your passion	Being Environmentally-Friendly	Gaps Can Be Good: The Advantages of a Gap Year
look for … in	Competing in the Job Market	What Does "IT" Really Mean?
be/get used to	Using Technology in Your Daily Life	Escape to India —Through Movies!
focus on	Promoting Your Own Culture	Why Is French Food So Good?
in the first place	Doing Volunteer Work	Can One Person Change the World?

About This Textbook

本書について

本書は、日本で働いている様々な国籍・業種の方々への取材と英語によるインタビュー撮影※を行い、その映像を活用したビデオ教材です。それぞれの業界で活躍する彼らの語る仕事観・日本観・人生観などは、皆さんの将来に役立つヒントに富み、積極的に興味深く英語を学ぶための最適な題材となっています。

※取材対象者に関する情報は2014年7月現在のものです。

ユニットごとに一人ずつ取り上げ、ビデオの視聴アクティビティを中心に学習が展開していきます。インタビューで使われている有用表現のスピーキング、インタビュー内容に関連したクリティカルシンキング、ユニットの最後には、取材に基づいて書き下ろしたエッセーのリーディングも用意してあります。

ビデオの基本構成

各ユニットのビデオはIntroductionとInterviewの2つのパートで構成されています。また、Interviewは理解しやすいように、内容別に3つのセクション（トピック）に分かれています。それぞれの映像の長さと主な内容は以下のとおりです。

▶ Introduction………取材対象者の紹介映像（約1分30秒）
▶ Interview……………ジャーナリスト Alice Gordenker による取材対象者へのインタビュー映像
    Topic 1：主に仕事の概要（約1分30秒）
    Topic 2：仕事や文化、ライフタイルなど様々な話題（約1分30秒）
    Topic 3：学生へ向けたアドバイスやメッセージ（約40秒）

Unit Walkthrough

ユニットの基本構成とアクティビティの特徴

各ユニットは6ページ構成です。以下に、それぞれのアクティビティの特徴とやり方を説明します。

[アイコンの説明]

DVD VIDEO DVDに収録のビデオ映像を使うアクティビティ。同じ映像をオンラインでも視聴できます。

DVD AUDIO DVDに収録のアクティビティ用のオーディオ音声。同じ音声をオンラインでも聴くことができます。

CD1 02 教師用CDにはDVDと同じビデオ音声とオーディオ音声を収録。
下の数字はCDのトラック番号を示しています。

Unit 1

Sales Can Be Like Acting

David White
Sales Representative, National Geographic Learning

Warm-up Look at the unit title and the picture above. Answer the questions below.

1. Why do you think this man has so many books?
2. Which country's flag is this? What are three things you know about this country?

Key Vocabulary Match each word/phrase with the correct meaning.

[　] 1. deal (n.)
[　] 2. improvise (v.)
[　] 3. memorize (v.)
[　] 4. on the road (ph.)
[　] 5. opportunity (n.)
[　] 6. patient (adj.)
[　] 7. publisher (n.)
[　] 8. recommend (v.)
[　] 9. role (n.)
[　] 10. sales representative (n.)

a. remember something without looking at notes
b. traveling from place to place
c. a company which produces and sells books
d. a good chance or position for success
e. not in a rush; able or willing to wait for something
f. tell others that something is good
g. perform or do suddenly without preparation
h. a person's function or part at work or in a movie
i. a business decision or agreement
j. a person who sell products for a company

12

Warm-up

ユニットで取り上げる取材対象者に関する問題。クイズ感覚で楽しみながら質問に答えましょう。

1. 写真やユニットタイトルを見て、どんな仕事をしているか想像してみましょう。名前の下に記載の職種名（肩書）や所属先（会社・団体）をヒントにするのもよいでしょう。
2. 国籍を示す旗を見て、その国名を答えましょう。次に、その国について自分が知っていることを3つ挙げてみましょう。

Key Vocabulary

ビデオに出てくる重要語句10個を提示。それぞれの意味を選んで答えましょう。

DVD AUDIO 各語句のモデル発音を収録。ビデオ視聴前に、重要語句の発音を確認しましょう。

📽 Introduction

ユニットで取り上げる取材対象者の紹介映像を2回視聴し、それぞれ形式の異なる問題に答えながら内容を理解しましょう。

DVD VIDEO ビデオを使うアクティビティ。

First Viewing

紹介映像を視聴し、4枚の写真に対してビデオ登場順に番号を振る問題。写真の下（右）の英文をヒントにしてみましょう。まずは細部をあまり気にせず、リラックスしながら楽しく映像を視聴してください。

Second Viewing

もう一度紹介映像を視聴し、出身国や経歴の空所を埋めて、取材対象者のプロフィールを完成する問題。2回目は細部に注意して視聴し、番号の付いた空所には枠内から単語を選んで入れ、アルファベットの付いた空所には数字や年号を入れましょう。

📽 Introduction

Sales Can Be Like Acting **Unit 1**

DVD VIDEO

First Viewing Watch the Introduction. Number the pictures in the order in which they appear.

a. David visits schools for his job.
b. David has lived in the hometown of The Beatles.
c. David used to be an actor.
d. David has a job connected with books.

Second Viewing Watch the Introduction again. Fill in the missing information in David's profile. In [1]–[8], write the correct words from the box. In [a], write the correct number.

Name: David White   **Home country:**
Job: sales representative

Background & Career:
- David works for a [¹　　　] of English-learning [²　　　].
- He [³　　　] to many schools in Japan and recommends [⁴　　　] to teachers for their classes.
- He grew up in [⁵　　　], but moved to [⁶　　　] when he was [ᵃ　　　].
- Before coming to Japan, he traveled around the world, playing many [⁷　　　] as an actor.
- He did a kind of theater called "comedy [⁸　　　]."

Birmingham
improvisation
Liverpool
materials
publisher
roles
textbooks
travels

13

Interview

Alice Gordenker による取材対象者へのインタビュー映像をトピックごとに3つに分けて視聴。各トピックのインタビュー映像を2回ずつ視聴し、それぞれ形式の異なる問題に答えながら内容を理解しましょう。

Predicting

インタビュー映像の視聴前に、各トピックのタイトルからそれぞれのインタビューで語られるテーマや内容を推測する問題。事前に内容をイメージしておくことで、インタビューを理解しやすくなります。

TOPIC 1 & 2

First Viewing

インタビューを視聴し、Alice または取材対象者、どちらか一方の4つの発言に対して語った順に番号を振る問題。まずは細部をあまり気にせず、リラックスしながら映像を視聴し、インタビューの大意の把握に努めましょう。

Second Viewing

もう一度インタビューを視聴し、択一形式または True or False 形式の問題に答えながら、内容をより深く理解しましょう。2回目は細部に注意して視聴する必要があります。

TOPIC 3

First Viewing

インタビューを視聴し、取材対象者の3つの発言（スクリプト）を完成させる問題。空所には単語を入れますが、与えられていないので、注意して視聴する必要があります。

Second Viewing

もう一度インタビューを視聴し、内容の要約を完成させる問題。空所には枠内から単語を選んで入れましょう。与えられている単語の中にはインタビューに直接は出てこないものや時制が異なるものもあります。

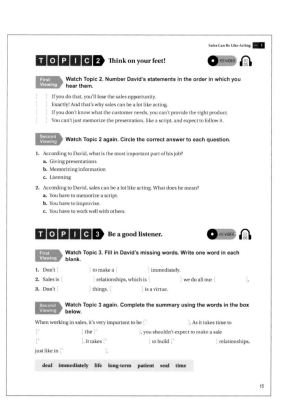

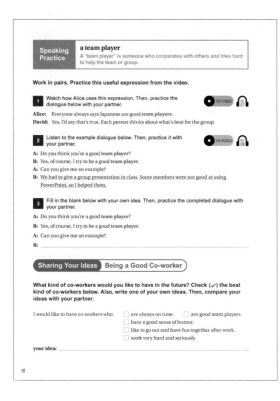

Speaking Practice

インタビューで使われている便利な表現を1つ取り上げ、ペアでスピーキング練習を3段階で行います。

....

1 表現が使われている対話部分のインタビュー映像を視聴し、ペアで練習。

2 **1**とは別の状況で同じ表現を使ったモデル会話の音声を聴き、ペアで練習。

3 **2**の会話の一部を自分の考えや意見に置き換え、完成した会話をペアで練習。

Sharing Your Ideas

インタビューの内容に即したテーマを取り上げ、それについての質問を提示。選択肢から選んだり考え出したりして、自分の回答を完成させましょう。また、その回答をパートナーと比較してみましょう。

Reading Passage

長文読解。本文は200語前後で、取材対象者やインタビューの内容に関連した興味深いトピックを厳選。英字新聞『ジャパンタイムズ』のコラムなどで好評を博している軽快なタッチの易しいエッセーを読み、2種類の問題に答えましょう。

 本文のナレーション音声を収録。

Comprehension Check

True or False 形式の内容理解問題。文章の流れに沿って出題しているので、すばやく要点を理解できます。

Your Opinions

本文の内容を踏まえつつ、自分の意見や経験を表す英文を提示。自分に合うほうの選択肢を丸で囲み、各英文を完成させます。完成した自分の意見をパートナーと比較してみましょう。

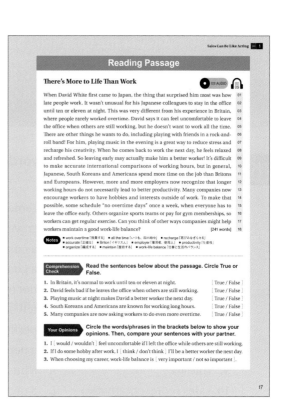

Sales Can Be Like Acting

David White
Sales Representative, National Geographic Learning

Warm-up	Look at the unit title and the picture above. Answer the questions below.

1. Why do you think this man has so many books?
2. Which country's flag is this? What are three things you know about this country?

Key Vocabulary	Match each word/phrase with the correct meaning.

[ ] **1.** deal (n.)   **a.** remember something without looking at notes

[ ] **2.** improvise (v.)   **b.** traveling from place to place

[ ] **3.** memorize (v.)   **c.** a company which produces and sells books

[ ] **4.** on the road (ph.)   **d.** a good chance or position for success

[ ] **5.** opportunity (n.)   **e.** not in a rush; able or willing to wait for something

[ ] **6.** patient (adj.)   **f.** tell others that something is good

[ ] **7.** publisher (n.)   **g.** perform or do suddenly without preparation

[ ] **8.** recommend (v.)   **h.** a person's function or part at work or in a movie

[ ] **9.** role (n.)   **i.** a business decision or agreement

[ ] **10.** sales representative (n.)   **j.** a person who sell products for a company

Introduction

First Viewing Watch the Introduction. Number the pictures in the order in which they appear.

David visits schools for his job.

David has lived in the hometown of The Beatles.

David used to be an actor.

David has a job connected with books.

Second Viewing Watch the Introduction again. Fill in the missing information in David's profile. In [1]–[8], write the correct words from the box. In [a], write the correct number.

Name: David White   **Home country:** _____

Job: sales representative _____

Background & Career:

- David works for a [1. _____] of English-learning [2. _____].

- He [3. _____] to many schools in Japan and recommends [4. _____] to teachers for their classes.

- He grew up in [5. _____], but moved to [6. _____] when he was [a. _____].

- Before coming to Japan, he traveled around the world, playing many [7. _____] as an actor.

- He did a kind of theater called "comedy [8. _____]."

Birmingham
improvisation
Liverpool
materials
publisher
roles
textbooks
travels

Interview

Predicting Read the titles of Topics 1–3 below. What do you think each title means? Write your own ideas. Then, compare your ideas with a partner.

Topic 1: Play your role well.

Topic 2: Think on your feet!

Topic 3: Be a good listener.

T O P I C 1 Play your role well.

First Viewing Watch Topic 1. Number Alice's questions or statements in the order in which you hear them.

[   ]   Everyone always says Japanese are good team players.
[   ]   What kind of work are you doing then?
[   ]   Are you comfortable working in an office where everyone else is Japanese?
[   ]   So each member of the team has a role to play.

Second Viewing Watch Topic 1 again. Circle True or False.

1. David travels for work especially in summer.   [True / False]
2. David spends a lot of time in the office, too.   [True / False]
3. Part of David's job is to collect and review sales data.   [True / False]
4. David enjoys working in an office with all Japanese people.   [True / False]
5. In the office, Japanese people think of themselves first.   [True / False]

T O P I C 2 Think on your feet!

First Viewing Watch Topic 2. Number David's statements in the order in which you hear them.

[   ] If you do that, you'll lose the sales opportunity.

[   ] Exactly! And that's why sales can be a lot like acting.

[   ] If you don't know what the customer needs, you can't provide the right product.

[   ] You can't just memorize the presentation, like a script, and expect to follow it.

Second Viewing Watch Topic 2 again. Circle the correct answer to each question.

1. According to David, what is the most important part of his job?
   a. Giving presentations
   b. Memorizing information
   c. Listening

2. According to David, sales can be a lot like acting. What does he mean?
   a. You have to memorize a script.
   b. You have to improvise.
   c. You have to work well with others.

T O P I C 3 Be a good listener.

First Viewing Watch Topic 3. Fill in David's missing words. Write one word in each blank.

1. Don't [   ] to make a [   ] immediately.

2. Sales is [   ] relationships, which is [   ] we do all our [   ].

3. Don't [   ] things. [   ] is a virtue.

Second Viewing Watch Topic 3 again. Complete the summary using the words in the box below.

When working in sales, it's very important to be [1.   ]. As it takes time to [2.   ] the [3.   ], you shouldn't expect to make a sale [4.   ]. It takes [5.   ] to build [6.   ] relationships, just like in [7.   ].

deal	immediately	life	long-term	patient	seal	time

a team player

A "team player" is someone who cooperates with others and tries hard to help the team or group.

Work in pairs. Practice this useful expression from the video.

1 Watch how Alice uses this expression. Then, practice the dialogue below with your partner.

DVD VIDEO CD1 07

Alice: Everyone always says Japanese are good **team players**.

David: Yes, I'd say that's true. Each person thinks about what's best for the group.

2 Listen to the example dialogue below. Then, practice it with your partner.

DVD AUDIO CD1 08

A: Do you think you're a good **team player**?

B: Yes, of course. I try to be a good **team player**.

A: Can you give me an example?

B: We had to give a group presentation in class. Some members were not good at using PowerPoint, so I helped them.

3 Fill in the blank below with your own idea. Then, practice the completed dialogue with your partner.

A: Do you think you're a good **team player**?

B: Yes, of course. I try to be a good **team player**.

A: Can you give me an example?

B: _____

Sharing Your Ideas   Being a Good Co-worker

What kind of co-workers would you like to have in the future? Check (✓) the best kind of co-workers below. Also, write one of your own ideas. Then, compare your ideas with your partner.

I would like to have co-workers who: ☐ are always on time. ☐ are good team players.

☐ have a good sense of humor.

☐ like to go out and have fun together after work.

☐ work very hard and seriously.

your idea: _____.

Reading Passage

There's More to Life Than Work

When David White first came to Japan, the thing that surprised him most was how   01
late people work. It wasn't unusual for his Japanese colleagues to stay in the office   02
until ten or eleven at night. This was very different from his experience in Britain,   03
where people rarely worked overtime. David says it can feel uncomfortable to leave   04
the office when others are still working, but he doesn't want to work all the time.   05
There are other things he wants to do, including playing with friends in a rock-and-   06
roll band! For him, playing music in the evening is a great way to reduce stress and   07
recharge his creativity. When he comes back to work the next day, he feels relaxed   08
and refreshed. So leaving early may actually make him a better worker! It's difficult   09
to make accurate international comparisons of working hours, but in general,   10
Japanese, South Koreans and Americans spend more time on the job than Britons   11
and Europeans. However, more and more employers now recognize that longer   12
working hours do not necessarily lead to better productivity. Many companies now   13
encourage workers to have hobbies and interests outside of work. To make that   14
possible, some schedule "no overtime days" once a week, when everyone has to   15
leave the office early. Others organize sports teams or pay for gym memberships, so   16
workers can get regular exercise. Can you think of other ways companies might help   17
workers maintain a good work-life balance?   [241 words]   18

Notes
- work overtime「残業する」 ■ all the time「いつも、四六時中」 ■ recharge「再びみなぎらせる」
- accurate「正確な」 ■ Briton「イギリス人」 ■ employer「雇用者、使用人」 ■ productivity「生産性」
- organize「編成する」 ■ maintain「維持する」 ■ work-life balance「仕事と生活のバランス」

....

Comprehension Check   **Read the sentences below about the passage. Circle True or False.**

1. In Britain, it's normal to work until ten or eleven at night.   [True / False]
2. David feels bad if he leaves the office when others are still working.   [True / False]
3. Playing music at night makes David a better worker the next day.   [True / False]
4. South Koreans and Americans are known for working long hours.   [True / False]
5. Many companies are now asking workers to do even more overtime.   [True / False]

Your Opinions   **Circle the words/phrases in the brackets below to show your opinions. Then, compare your sentences with your partner.**

1. I [would / wouldn't] feel uncomfortable if I left the office while others are still working.
2. If I do some hobby after work, I [think / don't think] I'll be a better worker the next day.
3. When choosing my career, work-life balance is [very important / not so important].

Travel Opens Up the World

Merve Ozkok

Tour Planner, H.I.S.

Warm-up Look at the unit title and the picture above.
Answer the questions below.

1. What kind of job do you think this woman usually does?
2. Which country's flag is this? What are three things you know about this country?

Key Vocabulary Match each word/phrase with the correct meaning.

 DVD AUDIO

[   ] **1.** analyze (v.)   **a.** very interesting or special
[   ] **2.** branch (n.)   **b.** plan; prepare; coordinate
[   ] **3.** destination (n.)   **c.** a place people go to or visit
[   ] **4.** fascinating (adj.) **d.** one office of a company which has more than one location
[   ] **5.** infrastructure (n.) **e.** be careful that something happens or goes well
[   ] **6.** make sure (v.)   **f.** stop something from happening
[   ] **7.** organize (v.)   **g.** become bad; not go as planned
[   ] **8.** particularly (adv.) **h.** look at something carefully
[   ] **9.** prevent (v.)   **i.** especially; very much; one thing more than others
[   ] **10.** spoil (v.)   **j.** basic services such as transportation

Introduction

DVD VIDEO CD1 11

First Viewing — **Watch the Introduction. Number the pictures in the order in which they appear.**

a

Merve met the local H.I.S. branch manager in Istanbul.

b

Merve organized tours for Japanese people in Turkey.

c

Merve studied Japanese and visited Japan.

d

Merve was impressed by the H.I.S. company philosophy.

Second Viewing — **Watch the Introduction again. Fill in the missing information in Merve's profile. In [1]–[7], write the correct words from the box. In [a] and [b], write the correct number/year.**

Name: _Merve Ozkok_   **Home country:** _____

Job: _tour planner_ _____

Background & Career:

- Merve organizes tours for travel to [1. _____] and [2. _____] America.

- She is from Turkey, a fascinating country where [3. _____] meets [4. _____].

- For her graduation [5. _____], she compared the Japanese and Turkish [6. _____] industries.

- She worked for H.I.S. in Istanbul for [a. ____] years, but [7. _____] to Tokyo in [b. ____].

Central
East
South
thesis
transferred
travel
West

Interview

Predicting Read the titles of Topics 1–3 below. What do you think each title means? Write your own ideas. Then, compare your ideas with a partner.

Topic 1: Travel is all about dreams.

Topic 2: Big events bring big opportunities.

Topic 3: Travel makes life more fun.

TOPIC 1 Travel is all about dreams.

First Viewing Watch Topic 1. Number Alice's questions or statements in the order in which you hear them.

[   ] Speaking of dreams, what's your goal for the future?

[   ] You went the extra mile.

[   ] Was it your job to make those arrangements?

[   ] Is there one place you particularly recommend?

Second Viewing Watch Topic 1 again. Circle the correct answer to each question.

1. What does Merve do so that travelers can have nice vacations?

   a. She finds the best hotel rooms.

   b. She tries hard to speak Japanese.

   c. She checks everything again and again.

2. How does Merve feel about working for the travel industry?

   a. She wants to change jobs before she's 30.

   b. It's difficult, but she enjoys it.

   c. It's only good if you're a manager.

T O P I C **2** Big events bring big opportunities.

First Viewing Watch Topic 2. Number Merve's statements in the order in which you hear them.

[   ] Right now, Japan doesn't have the infrastructure to support so many visitors.

[   ] And if you join a travel business now, you'll be in a great position to do interesting work in 2020.

[   ] I'm planning tours and analyzing countries as possible new destinations.

[   ] We need wireless Internet that foreigners can access easily.

Second Viewing Watch Topic 2 again. Circle True or False.

1. Merve thinks Japan is ready for the 2020 Olympics. [True / False]
2. About 20 million people from overseas will visit Japan for the Olympics. [True / False]
3. Japan needs more wireless Internet to prepare for the Olympics. [True / False]
4. Japan already has enough signs in English now. [True / False]
5. Merve thinks it's a good time to join the travel business. [True / False]

T O P I C **3** Travel makes life more fun.

First Viewing Watch Topic 3. Fill in Merve's missing words. Write one word in each blank.

1. Learning [   ] [   ] makes life more fun.

2. You realize that there is [   ] to the [   ] than Japan.

3. And when you travel, you [   ] with people from different [   ].

Second Viewing Watch Topic 3 again. Complete the summary using the words in the box below.

You can [1.   ] many things through [2.   ]. First, you can [3.   ] and [4.   ] new things. You can also meet many kinds of [5.   ]. You will then understand that although we are [6.   ], we are also the [7.   ].

    different   gain   learn   people   same   see   travel

recommend

"Recommend" means to advise someone to do something because you think it is good.

Work in pairs. Practice this useful expression from the video.

1 Watch how Alice uses this expression. Then, practice the dialogue below with your partner.

`DVD VIDEO` `CD1 15`

Alice: In Istanbul, you organized tours all around Turkey. Is there one place you particularly **recommend**?

Merve: Cappadocia is very popular. You can ride in a hot air balloon over incredible scenery and stay in a cave hotel.

2 Listen to the example dialogue below. Then, practice it with your partner.

`DVD AUDIO` `CD1 16`

A: Millions of people from overseas will visit Japan for the 2020 Olympics. Is there one place you particularly **recommend** visiting in Japan?

B: I **recommend** visiting Hokkaido because it's very different from Tokyo. There will be so many people at the Olympics, but in Hokkaido they can see incredible natural scenery.

3 Fill in the blanks below with your own ideas. Then, practice the completed dialogue with your partner.

A: Millions of people from overseas will visit Japan for the 2020 Olympics. Is there one place you particularly **recommend** visiting in Japan?

B: I **recommend** visiting _____ because _____
_____ .

Sharing Your Ideas **Having Fun While Traveling**

There are many fun adventure activities you can try while traveling. Check (✓) the activity you would most like to try. Also, write one of your own ideas. Then, compare your ideas with your partner.

If I could try an adventure activity while traveling, I'd like to:

- ☐ go bungee jumping in New Zealand.
- ☐ go on a safari in Kenya.
- ☐ hike the Inca Trail to Machu Picchu in Peru.
- ☐ go cycling in Switzerland
- ☐ go scuba diving in Australia.
- ☐ ride in a hot air balloon in Turkey.

your idea: _____ .

Reading Passage

Japan Needs Muslim-Friendly Meals

Does your university cafeteria offer "halal" meals? An increasing number of 01
cafeterias at Japanese universities now offer halal items for Muslim students. In 02
Arabic, the word "halal" means "permitted" or "lawful." Halal foods are foods that 03
are permitted under Islamic dietary guidelines. You may already know that Muslims 04
are not supposed to eat pork or drink alcohol. However, following Islamic dietary 05
guidelines while living in Japan is more complicated than avoiding beer and *tonkatsu* 06
(pork cutlets). For example, did you know that *shoyu* (soy sauce) usually contains 07
small amounts of alcohol? Soy sauce is used in almost all Japanese cooking, which 08
makes it very difficult for Muslims to eat in restaurants in Japan. That's a shame 09
because they miss the many pleasures of *washoku* (Japanese cuisine). However, it is 10
possible to prepare Japanese food that meets Islamic dietary guidelines. You have to 11
use special soy sauce and follow certain rules. Many hotels and restaurants in Japan 12
are now learning how to prepare halal meals. That's great news for the increasing 13
number of Muslim tourists from countries such as Indonesia and Malaysia. It's also 14
important preparation for 2020, when Tokyo will host the Olympic and Para-Olympic 15
games. Many Muslim athletes and spectators will come to Japan for the games, and 16
they'll all need to eat!   [214 words] 17

Notes
- Muslim-friendly meals「イスラム教徒向けの食事」 ■ Arabic「アラビア語」 ■ permit「許可する」
- lawful「合法の」 ■ dietary「食べ物の、規定食の」 ■ be supposed to *do*「…することになっている」
- complicated「複雑な」 ■ avoid「避ける」 ■ contain「含む」 ■ amount「量」
- That's a shame.「残念なことだ、もったいない」 ■ pleasure「楽しみ」 ■ meet「見合う」 ■ follow「従う」
- spectator「観客」

Comprehension Check   **Read the sentences below about the passage. Circle True or False.**

1. Some Japanese university cafeterias now have halal items. [True / False]
2. Halal food means that all dishes are vegetarian. [True / False]
3. Most soy sauce contains alcohol. [True / False]
4. Japanese food can never meet Islamic dietary guidelines. [True / False]
5. Hotels and restaurants in Japan should learn to prepare halal meals. [True / False]

Your Opinions   **Circle the words/phrases in the brackets below to show your opinions. Then, compare your sentences with your partner.**

1. I [had / had not] heard of halal food before reading this passage.
2. For me, avoiding eating pork would be [very difficult / not so difficult].
3. In my opinion, Tokyo is [ready / not ready] for the 2020 Olympics.

Love Sells Cars

Tiziana Alamprese
Marketing Director, Fiat Chrysler Japan

Warm-up **Look at the unit title and the picture above. Answer the questions below.**

1. This woman has a job related to cars. What do you think she does?
2. Which country's flag is this? What are three things you know about this country?

Key Vocabulary **Match each word/phrase with the correct meaning.**

[   ] **1.** awareness (n.)   **a.** do something creatively, uniquely, differently
[   ] **2.** contribution (n.)   **b.** get someone to move somewhere
[   ] **3.** crush (v.)   **c.** design or idea for reaching a goal or target
[   ] **4.** drive (v.)   **d.** understanding or knowledge of something
[   ] **5.** encourage (v.)   **e.** destroy; break
[   ] **6.** manage (v.)   **f.** something that is given
[   ] **7.** share (v.)   **g.** tell or guide other workers about what they should do
[   ] **8.** strategy (n.)   **h.** help others feel they can do something
[   ] **9.** track (v.)   **i.** keep a record of something
[   ] **10.** think outside the box (v.) **j.** do or use something together with others

Introduction

First Viewing — Watch the Introduction. Number the pictures in the order in which they appear.

Tiziana received an award.

Tiziana works for a car company.

Tiziana's family car was a Fiat.

Tiziana studied at a Japanese university.

Second Viewing — Watch the Introduction again. Fill in the missing information in Tiziana's profile. In [1]–[6], write the correct words from the box. In [a] and [b], write the correct years.

Name: Tiziana Alamprese   **Home country:** _____

Job: marketing director

Background & Career:

- As a teenager, Tiziana became interested in Zen [1. _____].
- She learned [2. _____] at a university in Naples that is famous for [3. _____] studies.
- She studied [4. _____] at Kyushu University.
- In [a. _____], she came back to [5. _____] and started to work for Fiat.
- In [b. _____], she received an award from the [6. _____] government for her contributions to Italian-Japanese relations.

Asian
Italian
economics
Japan
Japanese
philosophy

Interview

Predicting **Read the titles of Topics 1–3 below. What do you think each title means? Write your own ideas. Then, compare your ideas with a partner.**

Topic 1: A brand is like a baby.

Topic 2: Sharing creates happiness.

Topic 3: Give yourself a smile.

T O P I C 1 A brand is like a baby.

First Viewing **Watch Topic 1. Number Alice's questions in the order in which you hear them.**

[   ] But really—what is "marketing"?

[   ] How do you encourage your team to think outside the box?

[   ] Numbers are important. What else is necessary?

[   ] Wow. How do you manage five different brands?

Second Viewing **Watch Topic 1 again. Circle the correct answer to each question.**

1. How does Tiziana explain the meaning of "marketing"?
   a. Making people know your products
   b. Making people try your products
   c. Making people love and buy your products

2. What is Tiziana's management style?
   a. She seems to be serious and quiet.
   b. She seems to be creative and fun.
   c. She seems to get angry easily.

T O P I C **2** Sharing creates happiness.

First Viewing Watch Topic 2. Number Tiziana's statements in the order in which you hear them.

[   ] When I started this job, awareness of our brand was very low in Japan.

[   ] It's through sharing that we create true happiness for everyone.

[   ] It was the first car café in Japan.

[   ] We love to share the space with the NPOs that we support.

Second Viewing Watch Topic 2 again. Circle True or False.

1. The Fiat Caffè was the first car café in Japan.   [True / False]
2. Women in Japan enjoy going to car showrooms.   [True / False]
3. In Japan, women buy more than half of Fiat's cars.   [True / False]
4. Fiat shares their space with many NPOs.   [True / False]
5. Tiziana thinks our own happiness is most important.   [True / False]

T O P I C **3** Give yourself a smile.

First Viewing Watch Topic 3. Fill in Tiziana's missing words. Write one word in each blank.

1. I take a picture of myself with a [   ] [   ] on my face.

2. Because you have to [   ] [   ] [   ] yourself. You have to love yourself.

3. Of course I have [   ]. But I don't let them [   ] me.

Second Viewing Watch Topic 3 again. Complete the summary using the words in the box below.

Tiziana wants to keep herself [1.   ] even when she has [2.   ], so she takes a picture of herself [3.   ] every [4.   ]. She advises that you have to [5.   ] yourself because you will be [6.   ] by others if you [7.   ] yourself.

| love   morning   positive   respect   respected   smiling   troubles |

What's your secret?

"What's your secret?" is another way of asking someone how he/she became good or successful at something.

Work in pairs. Practice this useful expression from the video.

1 Watch how Alice uses this expression. Then, practice the dialogue below with your partner.

DVD VIDEO | CD1 23

Alice: You have a really tough job but you always seem so positive. **What's your secret?**

Tiziana: Ah, it's my "Smile Project." Every morning, I take a picture of myself with a big smile on my face.

2 Listen to the example dialogue below. Then, practice it with your partner.

DVD AUDIO | CD1 24

A: I'm good at speaking English.

B: Wow, **what's your secret?**

A: I practice speaking English as much as I can outside of class.

3 Fill in the blanks below with your own ideas. Then, practice the completed dialogue with your partner.

A: I'm good at _____.

B: Wow, **what's your secret?**

A: _____

Sharing Your Ideas | Staying Positive

What is the best way to have a positive, less stressful life? Check (✓) the best way below. Also, write one of your own ideas. Then, compare your ideas with your partner.

The best way to stay positive is to:
- ☐ eat something you love every day.
- ☐ exercise regularly.
- ☐ go shopping on weekends.
- ☐ go to karaoke.
- ☐ get enough sleep.
- ☐ spend a lot of time with family/friends.

your idea: _____.

Reading Passage

Money Isn't Everything

Do you think corporations exist only to make money? Or do you think companies 01
should try to make the world a better place? Like many people today, Tiziana 02
Alamprese believes companies should "give back" to the communities where they do 03
business, an idea that is called "corporate social responsibility." How can a company 04
"give back" to society? The company where Tiziana works, Fiat Chrysler Japan, 05
supports 18 non-profit organizations (NPOs) in Japan. One is the Japan Blind Football 06
Association (JBFA), which organizes soccer games for people who cannot see. By 07
using a special ball that makes noise, players can locate it by sound. It's wonderful 08
that sports can be adapted so everyone can play. Another group the company 09
supports created jobs for women who lost everything in the Great East Japan 10
Earthquake. Just months after the disaster, the women were able to earn money by 11
making Christmas ornaments that were sold in the Fiat Caffé in Tokyo. Fiat supports 12
the NPOs not only with direct donations, but also by organizing joint events to help 13
raise awareness of their missions and activities. How do employees at Fiat feel about 14
their company giving away money? Do they wish the company would give them 15
bigger salaries instead? Not at all. Employees say they like that the company supports 16
good causes. They feel proud to work for an Italian company that is helping people in 17
Japan.   [232 words] 18

Notes
- give back to「…に還元する」 ■ corporate social responsibility「企業の社会的責任」
- the Japan Blind Football Association「日本ブラインドサッカー協会」(blind は「目の不自由な」という意味)
- locate「…の位置を見つける」 ■ adapt「…を（目的に）合わせて変える」
- the Great East Japan Earthquake「東日本大震災」 ■ disaster「災害」 ■ good cause「大義、正当な理由」

Comprehension Check Read the sentences below about the passage. Circle True or False.

1. Tiziana believes that the only purpose of companies is to make money. [True / False]
2. Fiat donates money and organizes events for different charities. [True / False]
3. Players in the JBFA know where the ball is because of the sound it makes. [True / False]
4. Fiat helped women after the Great East Japan Earthquake by giving them money. [True / False]

Your Opinions Circle the words/phrases in the brackets below to show your opinions. Then, compare your sentences with your partner.

1. For me, money [is / isn't] everything.
2. I think it's [important / not so important] for companies to give back to society.
3. When I join a company, salary is [very important / not so important].

Translating Is More Than Words

Alexander O. Smith

Translator, Kajiya Productions

Warm-up **Look at the unit title and the picture above. Answer the questions below.**

1. Why are these books important or special to this man?
2. Which country's flag is this? What are three things you know about this country?

Key Vocabulary **Match each word/phrase with the correct meaning.**

 DVD AUDIO CD1 26

[   ] **1.** come across (v.)   **a.** manage; operate a business
[   ] **2.** context (n.)   **b.** start; create
[   ] **3.** explore (v.)   **c.** level of education after university
[   ] **4.** express (v.)   **d.** good point; a thing you are good at
[   ] **5.** graduate school (n.)   **e.** change from one language to another
[   ] **6.** recreate (v.)   **f.** say; show
[   ] **7.** run (v.)   **g.** look for; try to find something
[   ] **8.** set up (v.)   **h.** make again in a new way
[   ] **9.** strength (n.)   **i.** find; see; discover
[   ] **10.** translate (v.)   **j.** information that helps you understand something

Introduction

First
Viewing

Watch the Introduction. Number the pictures in the order in which they appear.

Alex's parents ran a hotel.

Alex is a father.

Alex works on books and games.

Alex loved role-playing games as a child.

Second
Viewing

Watch the Introduction again. Fill in the missing information in Alex's profile. In [1]–[7], write the correct words from the box.

Name: Alexander Smith   **Home country:** _____

Job: translator

Background & Career:

- Alex worked at Square Enix and then set up his own
  [1.   ] agency.
- He now [2.   ] books and video games from
  [3.   ] into [4.   ].
- As a child, he loved [5.   ] role-playing games and even
  wrote his own games.
- His parents ran a hotel and [6.   ] came from all over the
  world.
- He was an exchange student in [7.   ] in high school.

| China |
| fantasy |
| guests |
| translates |
| translation |
| English |
| Japanese |

 # Interview

 Predicting Read the titles of Topics 1–3 below. What do you think each title means? Write your own ideas. Then, compare your ideas with a partner.

Topic 1: Learn your strengths.

_____

Topic 2: You have to translate the experience.

_____

Topic 3: Sometimes plans change.

_____

T O P I C 1 Learn your strengths.

First Viewing Watch Topic 1. Number Alice's questions or statements in the order in which that you hear them.

[   ]   Would that work for learning English, too?
[   ]   So, you had a wide range of experiences.
[   ]   How did you learn Japanese so well?
[   ]   You mean, how the words are used?

Second Viewing Watch Topic 1 again. Circle the correct answer to each question.

1. According to Alex, what is the best way to learn a language?
    a. Using the dictionary   **b.** Studying words in context   **c.** Playing video games

2. How would you describe Alex?
    a. He is nervous and shy.   **b.** He likes to relax a lot.   **c.** He likes new challenges.

T O P I C 2   You have to translate the experience.

First Viewing **Watch Topic 2. Number Alex's statements in the order in which you hear them.**

[   ]   It means recreating the game in another culture.

[   ]   But with games we don't call it "translating." We call it "localizing."

[   ]   You have to translate the experience.

[   ]   The scene would have lost its power.

Second Viewing **Watch Topic 2 again. Circle True or False.**

1. Translating video games is called "localizing." [True / False]

2. "Localizing" means remaking a game to make it understood in different cultures.

[True / False]

3. Alex designed the game Final Fantasy X. [True / False]

4. In the English version of Final Fantasy X, the boy says "Thank you." [True / False]

5. English is a more direct language than Japanese. [True / False]

T O P I C 3   Sometimes plans change.

First Viewing **Watch Topic 3. Fill in Alex's missing words. Write one word in each blank.**

1. No, because I knew my [   ].

2. I was good at [   ]. I was good at [   ].

3. If you [   ] your interests, you'll find your [   ].

Second Viewing **Watch Topic 3 again. Complete the summary using the words in the box below.**

Although he wanted to be a [1.   ], Alex changed his plan during

[2.   ] school. Still, such a change wasn't [3.   ]. Because

Alex knew his [4.   ], he could find the right [5.   ]. After

all, everyone is good at [6.   ].

career	**graduate**	**professor**	**scary**	**something**	**strengths**

explore different interests

"Explore different interests" is another way of saying that you are trying to learn more about many things.

Work in pairs. Practice this useful expression from the video.

1 Watch how Alex uses this expression. Then, practice the dialogue below with your partner.

DVD VIDEO   CD1 31

Alice: So, you had a wide range of experiences.
Alex: College is a great place to **explore different interests**.

2 Listen to the example dialogue below. Then, practice it with your partner.

DVD AUDIO   CD1 32

A: College is a good place to **explore different interests**.
B: That's true. In college, I joined a guitar circle.
A: Oh, why did you decide to do that?
B: Because I love the sound of the guitar, so I wanted to learn to play.

3 Fill in the blanks below with your own ideas. Then, practice the completed dialogue with your partner.

A: College is a good place to **explore different interests**.
B: That's true. In college, I _____.
A: Oh, why did you decide to do that?
B: Because _____.

Sharing Your Ideas   Learning Foreign Languages

What do you think is the best way to learn a foreign language well? Check (✓) the best way below. Also, write one of your own ideas. Then, compare your ideas with your partner.

I think the best way to learn a foreign language well is to:

☐ listen to music in that language.
☐ practice speaking with many people in that language.
☐ read many books, newspapers, or magazines in that language.
☐ use the dictionary to study that language.
☐ watch TV shows and movies in that language.

your idea: _____.

Reading Passage

Why Learn Japanese?

Have you ever wondered why someone decides to learn Japanese? For many people, an interest in Japanese culture provides the initial spark. Some people study Japanese because of an interest in martial arts, tea ceremony or kabuki. For others, the draw is often some aspect of popular culture, like manga, fashion or J-Pop. But for American translator Alexander O. Smith, it was an airplane menu that made him decide to learn Japanese. Yes, you read that right! It happened when Alex was a high school student, on his way back to the U.S. after six months in China as an exchange student. He had to change planes at Narita Airport, and on the plane from Tokyo, a flight attendant handed him a menu written in English, Chinese and Japanese. Alex eagerly compared how foods were written in each of the three languages. In Chinese, loanwords from English (like "salad" and "dessert") were written in complicated characters. But in Japanese, they were written in something simpler. Alex didn't know it then, but that writing was *katakana*, a syllabary used for loanwords, foreign names and for emphasis. Alex thought that was a much better system. In fact, he thought *katakana* were really cool, and decided then and there that he would study Japanese. You never know what will set you off on a new path.

01
02
03
04
05
06
07
08
09
10
11
12
13
14
15
[224 words] 16

Notes
- initial spark「最初のきっかけ」 - martial arts「武道」 - tea ceremony「茶道」 - draw「惹きつけるもの」
- aspect「側面」 - loanword「外来語」 - complicated character「複雑な文字」 - syllabary「音節文字」
- emphasis「強調」 - then and there「その場ですぐに」 - set ... off「…に着想を与える」 - path「方向、生き方」

Comprehension Check **Read the sentences below about the passage. Circle True or False.**

1. Many people start studying Japanese because of an interest in Japanese culture.

[True / False]

2. Alex started studying Japanese because of his interest in manga and J-Pop.

[True / False]

3. Alex was an exchange student in Tokyo.　　　　　　　　　　　　　[True / False]

4. Loanwords are written the same way in Chinese and Japanese.　　　[True / False]

5. Alex started to study Japanese because he thought *katakana* were cool.　[True / False]

Your Opinions **Circle the words/phrases in the brackets below to show your opinions. Then, compare your sentences with your partner.**

1. I'm more interested in [traditional / popular] Japanese culture.

2. I [would / would not] like to be an exchange student someday.

3. I imagine Japanese is a [difficult / not so difficult] language for people to learn.

Serve Up the Best Possible Service

Lam Thanh Huyen
Assistant Supervisor, Lawson

Warm-up **Look at the unit title and the picture above. Answer the questions below.**

1. This woman works at Lawson. What do you think she does there?
2. Which country's flag is this? What are three things you know about this country?

Key Vocabulary **Match each word/phrase with the correct meaning.**

[   ] **1.** consideration (n.)   **a.** a person who checks work done by others

[   ] **2.** convince (v.)   **b.** about one person; not a group

[   ] **3.** in charge (ph.)   **c.** feeling that you can't finish or decide something

[   ] **4.** individual (adj.)   **d.** give or offer

[   ] **5.** interact (v.)   **e.** making a lot of money; good for business

[   ] **6.** profitable (adj.)   **f.** talk or communicate with others

[   ] **7.** provide (v.)   **g.** make someone think something is a good idea

[   ] **8.** supervisor (n.)   **h.** great; wonderful; very good

[   ] **9.** terrific (adj.)   **i.** having power over others

[   ] **10.** stuck (adj.)   **j.** showing care for others

Introduction

DVD VIDEO · CD1 35

First Viewing **Watch the Introduction. Number the pictures in the order in which they appear.**

Lam works as an assistant supervisor for Lawson.

Lam went to university in Japan.

Lam is learning important things at Lawson.

Lam has an older sister.

Second Viewing **Watch the Introduction again. Fill in the missing information in Lam's profile. In [1]–[8], write the correct words from the box. In [a], write the correct number.**

Name: Lam Thanh Huyen   **Home country:** _____

Job: assistant supervisor

Background & Career:

- Lam works for the [1.   ] store chain, Lawson. Her group is in charge of [a.   ] stores in [2.   ] Tokyo.
- She is [3.   ] and her older sister works in the foreign ministry in [4.   ].
- She decided to go to university in Oita because she could study both [5.   ] and [6.   ].
- She [7.   ] her parents to let her go to Japan because she [8.   ] to return to Vietnam one day.

central
convenience
convinced
English
Japanese
promised
Vietnam
Vietnamese

Interview

Predicting Read the titles of Topics 1–3 below. What do you think each title means? Write your own ideas. Then, compare your ideas with a partner.

Topic 1: Process information quickly.

_____

Topic 2: Show customers that you care.

_____

Topic 3: It's OK to ask for help.

_____

T O P I C **1** Process information quickly.

First Viewing Watch Topic 1. Number Lam's statements in the order in which you hear them.

[   ] That's the most difficult part of my job.

[   ] Every week, we introduce about 100 new products.

[   ] Convenience stores work on very small margins.

[   ] On Thursday and Friday, I visit stores to see how they are doing, and give them advice.

Second Viewing Watch Topic 1 again. Circle the correct answer to each question.

1. What kind of work schedule does Lam have?
   a. She does the same kind of work every day.
   b. She has to do different things on different days of the week.
   c. She always has to work at night and on weekends.

2. According to Lam, what is the most difficult part of her job?
   a. Processing information very quickly
   b. Working in a foreign language
   c. Convincing store managers to listen to her

T O P I C **2**   Show customers that you care.

First Viewing   **Watch Topic 2. Number Alice's questions or statements in the order in which you hear them.**

[   ]   Coffee is that important?

[   ]   Consideration. To show them that you care.

[   ]   Even in a convenience store, you're providing individual customer service.

[   ]   Terrific customer service. That's one reason I love Japan.

Second Viewing   **Watch Topic 2 again. Circle True or False.**

1. The first thing Lam does at work is drink a cup of coffee.   [True / False]
2. Coffee is the most profitable item at Lawson.   [True / False]
3. At the "MACHI Café" corner, Lam checks only the taste of the coffee. [True / False]
4. Lam thinks having conversations with customers is important.   [True / False]
5. Lam wants to introduce Japanese customer service to Vietnam.   [True / False]

T O P I C **3**   It's OK to ask for help.

First Viewing   **Watch Topic 3. Fill in Lam's missing words. Write one word in each blank.**

1. She helped me [   ] that I love [   ] with people.

2. I've got the right [   ] for customer [   ].

3. If you're [   ] [   ], it's OK to ask for help.

Second Viewing   **Watch Topic 3 again. Complete the summary using the words in the box below.**

Lam didn't [1.   ] she wanted to work in the [2.   ]

industry at first. Although she interviewed with [3.   ] and

[4.   ] companies, she didn't get any [5.   ].

However, her teacher gave her good [6.   ] and she

[7.   ] that customer service was right for her.

> **advice   know   manufacturers   offers   realized   service   trading**

the rest of

"The rest of" means the remainder or final part of something.

Work in pairs. Practice this useful expression from the video.

1 Watch how Alice uses this expression. Then, practice the dialogue below with your partner.

DVD VIDEO   CD1 39

Alice: How about **the rest of** your week?

Lam: On Thursday and Friday, I visit stores to see how they are doing, and give them advice.

2 Listen to the example dialogue below. Then, practice it with your partner.

DVD AUDIO   CD1 40

A: If you could go anywhere, where would you like to spend **the rest of** your vacation?

B: I'd like to spend **the rest of** my vacation in Hokkaido.

A: Really? How come?

B: I'd like to spend **the rest of** my vacation in Hokkaido because I don't like hot weather. Hokkaido has cooler summers than other parts of Japan.

3 Fill in the blanks below with your own ideas. Then, practice the completed dialogue with your partner.

A: If you could go anywhere, where would you like to spend **the rest of** your vacation?

B: If I could go anywhere, I'd like to spend **the rest of** my vacation in _____.

A: Really? How come?

B: I'd like to spend **the rest of** my vacation in _____ because _____
_____.

Sharing Your Ideas   What Do You Love About Japan?

What do you love most about Japan? Check (✓) the thing you love the most below. Also, write one of your own ideas. Then, compare your ideas with your partner.

What I love the most about Japan is:

☐ the customer service.   ☐ the food.   ☐ seasonal events and festivals.

☐ traditional Japanese culture (tea ceremony, kimono, kabuki, etc.).

☐ modern Japanese pop culture (manga, anime, J-pop, etc.).

☐ the public transportation system (Shinkansen, etc.).

your idea: _____.

Reading Passage

Kisetsukan: "Sense of the Seasons" as a Marketing Tool

Imagine that you are in a store and see an interesting product. If you know the `01`
product will only be available for a short time, are you more likely to buy it? Most `02`
consumers respond to advertising phrases such as *kikan gentei* (limited-time offer) `03`
or *kisetsu gentei* (seasonal limited edition). In addition, many consumers in Japan, `04`
particularly women, enjoy buying products that carry a sense of the season, which `05`
is expressed in Japanese as *kisetsukan*. One recent example of a popular seasonal `06`
product is cherry-flavored coffee drinks in the spring. There are even seasonal beers, `07`
sold in cans brightly decorated with autumn leaves or snowflakes. Part of Lam Thanh `08`
Huyen's job at Lawson is rotating such products in and out of convenience stores. She `09`
is impressed by the strong sense of the seasons in Japan because in Vietnam people `10`
pay less attention to changes in the seasons. Of course, there is a long tradition in `11`
Japan of observing and celebrating the changing seasons. In traditional poetry and `12`
literature, for example, there are special words called *kigo* that are associated with `13`
particular seasons. But today many Japanese live in cities where it's difficult to see `14`
how nature changes with the seasons. In modern Japan, is the sense of the seasons `15`
really linked to nature? Or is it created by marketing and advertising teams in order `16`
to sell more products?   [228 words] `17`

Notes ■ available「入手できる」 ■ consumer「消費者」 ■ respond to「…に反応する」 ■ particularly「特に」
■ cherry-flavored「桜の香りのついた」 ■ snowflake「雪の結晶」 ■ rotate「回転（循環）させる」
■ pay less attention to「（日本人ほど）…に気を留めない」 ■ observe「観察する」 ■ literature「文学」

Comprehension Check   **Read the sentences below about the passage. Circle True or False.**

1. Many Japanese want to buy products which have a sense of the season.   [True / False]
2. In Japan, the flavor of drinks can change from season to season.   [True / False]
3. In Vietnam, people pay a lot of attention to the change in the seasons.   [True / False]
4. Japan has a long history of paying attention to the change in the seasons.   [True / False]
5. These days, it's easy for most Japanese people to see the change of the seasons in
   nature.   [True / False]

Your Opinions   **Circle the words/phrases in the brackets below to show your opinions. Then, compare your sentences with your partner.**

1. Recently, I [have / haven't] bought a product which has a seasonal theme or flavor.
2. As for me, I pay [a lot of / little] attention to the changes in the seasons.
3. I think the four seasons [is / isn't] unique to Japan.

6

Toast Your Success!

Shigeharu Asagiri
President and CEO, Coedo Brewery

Warm-up	**Look at the unit title and the picture above. Answer the questions below.**

1. What kind of drink do you think this man makes?
2. What do you think the drink in the glass is made from?

Key Vocabulary	**Match each word/phrase with the correct meaning.**	

[　] **1.** brewery (n.)   **a.** a person who uses a product

[　] **2.** commitment (n.)   **b.** make a speech or announcement while raising drinks

[　] **3.** consumer (n.)   **c.** put something into the garbage

[　] **4.** craft (n.)   **d.** an award you get for doing something well

[　] **5.** domestic (adj.)   **e.** special skill or ability

[　] **6.** embarrassed (adj.)   **f.** a place where beer is made

[　] **7.** prize (n.)   **g.** trying something repeatedly in different ways

[　] **8.** throw out (v.)   **h.** feeling of making a mistake or doing something poorly

[　] **9.** toast (v.)   **i.** promise that you will do your best at something

[　] **10.** trial and error (n.) **j.** inside your own country

Introduction

DVD VIDEO   CD1 43

First Viewing   **Watch the Introduction. Number the pictures in the order in which they appear.**

Shigeharu grew up in Japan and attended local schools.

Shigeharu's company makes beer.

Shigeharu was amazed by the beers in Germany.

In university, Shigeharu backpacked abroad twice a year.

Second Viewing   **Watch the Introduction again. Fill in the missing information in Shigeharu's profile. In [1]–[8], write the correct words from the box.**

Name: _Shigeharu Asagiri_   **Hometown:** _____

Job: _president of a beer company_

Background & Career:

- Shigeharu's company makes [1.   ]-winning beers. They even make one from [2.   ] sweet potatoes!

- He had a [3.   ] upbringing in Japan and never lived or studied [4.   ] Japan.

- He studied [5.   ] and [6.   ] development at Hitotsubashi University.

- He now [7.   ] his own beers around the world and calls himself a "beer [8.   ]."

accounting
business
evangelist
local
outside
prize
ships
typical

🎥 Interview

Predicting   Read the titles of Topics 1–3 below. What do you think each title means? Write your own ideas. Then, compare your ideas with a partner.

Topic 1: Hard work pays off.

Topic 2: COEDO beer goes overseas.

Topic 3: Just try again.

T O P I C 1 ▶ Hard work pays off.

First Viewing   Watch Topic 1. Number Alice's questions or statements in the order in which you hear them.

[ ] Giving value to a product that would normally be thrown out.

[ ] Including Kawagoe's famous sweet potatoes?

[ ] Your hard work seems to have paid off.

[ ] And you redesigned your labels and marketing message, right?

Second Viewing   Watch Topic 1 again. Circle True or False.

1. Shigeharu copied the idea of using sweet potatoes from another brewery.   [True / False]
2. Shigeharu's company sold vegetables before making beer.   [True / False]
3. Finding a good recipe to make beer from sweet potatoes was easy.   [True / False]
4. Shigeharu's brewery makes 100 kinds of beer now.   [True / False]
5. Coedo is a small brewery.   [True / False]

T O P I C 2 COEDO beer goes overseas.

First Viewing Watch Topic 2. Number Shigeharu's statements or questions in the order in which you hear them.

[   ]   Winning international awards raised our profile in Japan dramatically.

[   ]   Do you know the Japanese word *monozukuri*?

[   ]   I'll go anywhere I have customers.

[   ]   Exports are about 15 percent of our business.

Second Viewing Watch Topic 2 again. Circle the correct answer to each question.

1. What is Shigeharu's business strategy?
   a. He wants to focus on the domestic market.
   b. He wants to focus on the international market.
   c. He wants to sell his beer wherever he can.

2. Why does Shigeharu think his beer has won international awards?
   a. It has a unique taste because it's made from sweet potatoes.
   b. They make hand-crafted, high-quality beer.
   c. They make a big variety of beers.

T O P I C 3 Just try again.

First Viewing Watch Topic 3. Fill in Shigeharu's missing words. Write one word in each blank.

1. It means I don't [   ] [   ].

2. Because I have [   ] I need to [   ].

3. If someone doesn't [   ] you the first time, don't [   ] embarrassed.

Second Viewing Watch Topic 3 again. Complete the summary using the words in the box below.

Shigeharu's advice about using English is to always keep [1.   ]. He has many

[2.   ] if someone doesn't understand his English. Sometimes he

[3.   ] a different [4.   ]. Other times he just [5.   ]

down what he [6.   ] to say. He also uses the [7.   ].

Internet   strategies   trying   uses   wants   word   writes

pay off

If something "pays off," there was a good result for hard work.

Work in pairs. Practice this useful expression from the video.

1 Watch how Alice uses this expression. Then, practice the dialogue below with your partner.

DVD VIDEO CD1 47

Alice: Your hard work seems to have **paid off**. We should toast your success.

Shigeharu: Thank you. Now we are one of the biggest small breweries in Japan.

2 Listen to the example dialogue below. Then, practice it with your partner.

DVD AUDIO CD1 48

A: Can you tell me about a time when your hard work **paid off**?

B: My hard work **paid off** when I prepared for the university entrance exam.

A: How did it **pay off**?

B: It **paid off** because I passed the entrance exam and got into university.

3 Fill in the blanks below with your own ideas. Then, practice the completed dialogue with your partner.

A: Can you tell me about a time when your hard work **paid off**?

B: My hard work **paid off** when I _____.

A: How did it **pay off**?

B: It **paid off** because _____.

Sharing Your Ideas   Making Your English Understood

What strategies would you use to make your English understood? Check (✓) the best strategy below. Also, write one of your own ideas. Then, compare your ideas with your partner.

If someone didn't understand my English, I would:

☐ draw a picture.

☐ try using a different word.

☐ use my dictionary.

☐ use the Internet or my smart phone.

☐ write down what I want to say.

your idea: _____.

Reading Passage

Think Global, Act Local

Shigeharu Asagiri likes to say that his company is a "glocal" business. But what does `01`
that mean? "Glocal" is a new word. It's a combination of "local" and "global" and `02`
comes from a slogan first used in 1969 by an American named David Brower, who `03`
founded an environmental group called Friends of the Earth. That slogan is "Think `04`
Global, Act Local." It means we should think on a global scale while taking action for `05`
positive change in our own local area. Shigeharu has adopted that way of thinking `06`
for his business. Shigeharu thinks globally, looking at the entire world. He buys the `07`
ingredients he needs to make beer not only from Japan, but from other countries `08`
as well. He markets his hand-crafted beers all around the world. At the same time, `09`
Shigeharu thinks locally—looking for ways he can help close to home. He supports `10`
local farmers by making beer from sweet potatoes that are too small for other uses. `11`
He also organizes an annual beer festival that brings many visitors to the local area. `12`
Some people think globalization is a good thing, because it brings opportunities `13`
such as jobs and development, as well as access to technology and medicines that `14`
can save lives. Others think globalization is harmful, because too much influence `15`
from other countries can harm local economies and cultures. Probably the truth lies `16`
somewhere in between. `[229 words]` `17`

Notes ■ environmental group「環境保護団体」 ■ adopt「採用する」 ■ ingredient「原料」
■ market「売り出す」 ■ save「救う」 ■ harmful「有害な」 ■ influence「影響」
■ harm「損害を与える」 ■ lie「位置する」 ■ in between「中間に」

Comprehension Check **Read the sentences below about the passage. Circle True or False.**

1. Shigeharu created the word "glocal." [True / False]
2. All the ingredients in Shigeharu's beer come from his local community. [True / False]
3. Shigeharu markets his beers both in Japan and internationally. [True / False]
4. Using sweet potatoes for his beer helps local farmers. [True / False]
5. According to the reading passage, globalization is always a good thing. [True / False]

Your Opinions **Circle the words/phrases in the brackets below to show your opinions. Then, compare your sentences with your partner.**

1. In my opinion, it's [very important / not so important] to support your local community.
2. I think beer made from sweet potatoes would taste [great / a little strange].
3. Overall, I think globalization is [a good thing / a bad thing] for Japan.

Unit 7

Teaching Is Helping Others Perform Their Best

Andrew Wakatsuki-Robinson
Teacher, Shukutoku Elementary School

Warm-up Look at the unit title and the picture above. Answer the questions below.

1. What kind of teacher do you think this man is? What subject do you think he teaches?
2. Which country's flag is this? What are three things you know about this country?

Key Vocabulary Match each word/phrase with the correct meaning.

[　] **1.** absorb (v.) **a.** say something good about or to a person

[　] **2.** adapt (v.) **b.** say something bad about or to a person

[　] **3.** competition (n.) **c.** something which makes us want to be or perform better

[　] **4.** cope with (v.) **d.** advise actors how to perform in a play or movie

[　] **5.** criticize (v.) **e.** be able to handle some challenge or difficulty

[　] **6.** direct (v.) **f.** relaxed; not too serious or strict

[　] **7.** laid-back (adj.) **g.** change something to fit a different situation or context

[　] **8.** motivator (n.) **h.** find something right or correct

[　] **9.** praise (v.) **i.** learn; remember

[　] **10.** prove (v.) **j.** trying to get ahead of someone else

Introduction

DVD VIDEO | CD1 51

First Viewing Watch the Introduction. Number the pictures in the order in which they appear.

a

Andrew majored in music.

b

Andrew directs theater.

c

Andrew grew up in a big family.

d

Andrew uses music in his teaching.

Second Viewing Watch the Introduction again. Fill in the missing information in Andrew's profile. In [1]–[7], write the correct words from the box. In [a], write the correct number.

Name: _Andrew Wakatsuki-Robinson_   **Home country:** _____

Job: _teacher_

Background & Career:

- Andrew teaches [1. _____] at an [2. _____] school in Tokyo.
- He comes from a family of [a. _____] children.
- In university, he studied [3. _____] and music and these things are still his [4. _____].
- In his free time, he directs theater and puts on [5. _____].
- Now he's [6. _____] Yamagata folk tales for the stage which will be [7. _____] in London.

adapting
elementary
English
passions
performed
plays
theater

49

 # Interview

 Predicting Read the titles of Topics 1–3 below. What do you think each title means? Write your own ideas. Then, compare your ideas with a partner.

Topic 1: Children learn in different ways.

_____

Topic 2: Give people options to try out.

_____

Topic 3: Don't tell; ask!

_____

T O P I C 1 Children learn in different ways.

First Viewing Watch Topic 1. Number Alice's questions or statements in the order in which you hear them.

[   ] You said, "teaching tools." Can you give me an example?
[   ] How do you keep your students' attention in the classroom?
[   ] That's two. What's the third?
[   ] How do you cope with so many different learning styles?

Second Viewing Watch Topic 1 again. Circle True or False.

1. All children learn in the same way.   [True / False]
2. Andrew uses many different tools in his teaching.   [True / False]
3. Music can make children want to learn new words.   [True / False]
4. Interacting with technology is a good way to learn. [True / False]
5. Competition is bad for children.   [True / False]

T O P I C **2** Give people options to try out.

First Viewing   Watch Topic 2. Number Andrew's statements in the order in which you hear them.

[   ] Teaching and directing are both about helping others perform their best.

[   ] I do the same thing in the classroom.

[   ] First, I look for something I can praise.

[   ] They are more likely to accept an idea if they've tested it themselves.

Second Viewing   Watch Topic 2 again. Circle the correct answer to each question.

1. How does Andrew feel about teaching children and directing adults?

   a. Teaching children is more difficult.

   b. Directing adults is more difficult.

   c. Teaching children or adults is the same thing.

2. What is Andrew's opinion about the best way to direct performers?

   a. The director should have full control.

   b. The director should let the performers make their own decisions.

   c. The director should criticize the performers a lot.

T O P I C **3** Don't tell; ask!

First Viewing   Watch Topic 3. Fill in Andrew's missing words. Write one word in each blank.

1. First of all, [   ] likes to be told they're doing something [   ].

2. Don't [   ]; instead, make a [   ] comment.

3. Next, ask questions, like, "What [   ] [   ] you do?"

Second Viewing   Watch Topic 3 again. Complete the summary using the words in the box below.

Nobody likes to be [1.   ], so it's important to praise them instead. People will find [2.   ] to [3.   ] their work if you help them see it more [4.   ]. After all, a teacher's job is to [5.   ] others [6.   ] their best.

| clearly | criticized | help | improve | perform | ways |

Speaking Practice

bring out the best in

"Bring out the best in" means to help someone become better or give a great performance.

Work in pairs. Practice this useful expression from the video.

1 Watch how Alice uses this expression. Then, practice the dialogue below with your partner.

DVD VIDEO CD1 55

Alice: How do you **bring out the best in** other people's performances?

Andrew: First, I look for something I can praise. I say something like, "I like the way you did that."

2 Listen to the example dialogue below. Then, practice it with your partner.

DVD AUDIO CD1 56

A: Who is someone who **brought out the best in** you?

B: My piano teacher **brought out the best in** me. She was great.

A: How did she do that?

B: She **brought out the best in** me by making me practice hard. Through hard practice, I could become better and better at playing the piano.

3 Fill in the blanks below with your own ideas. Then, practice the completed dialogue with your partner.

A: Who is someone who **brought out the best in** you?

B: _____ **brought out the best in** me. He/She was great.

A: How did he/she do that?

B: He/She **brought out the best in** me by _____

_____.

Sharing Your Ideas **Teaching English to Children**

What do you think is the best way to make children interested in English? Check (✓) the best way below. Also, write one of your own ideas. Then, compare your ideas with your partner.

I think the best way to make children interested in English is to:

☐ perform plays in English.　　☐ let children interact with technology in English.

☐ sing songs together in English.　　☐ play (competitive) games in English.

your idea: _____.

Reading Passage

Trouble for "Tall Poppies"

You are probably familiar with the Japanese proverb, *deru kui wa utareru*, which can be translated into English as "the nail that sticks up gets hammered down." The message of this proverb is, "If you stick out, people will criticize you." You may have seen this happen in your life in Japan, but did you know it happens in other countries, too? In New Zealand and Australia, people who are successful are sometimes called "tall poppies." This is not a compliment! Where did this expression come from? Imagine a garden. One flower is taller than all the others. What happens? The gardener cuts down the tall flower so it will be the same as all the others. The same thing may happen to people who are "tall poppies." Other people feel envious of the tall poppy, so they try to cut it down. The attacks are most often aimed at people who are seen as not deserving the success they've achieved. The tendency to attack successful people is called "Tall Poppy Syndrome." John Howard, the prime minister of Australia from 1996 to 2007, once said, "If there's one thing we need to get rid of in this country, it is our 'tall poppy syndrome.'" Why do you think he said that? What happens to a society when successful people are pulled down?   [222 words]

01 02 03 04 05 06 07 08 09 10 11 12 13 14 15

Notes
- poppy「ポピー（花の一種）」 ■ proverb「ことわざ、格言」 ■ nail「釘」
- stick up/out「突き出る」 ■ compliment「褒め言葉」 ■ feel envious of「…をねたましく思う」
- be aimed at「…に向けられる」 ■ deserve「…にふさわしい」 ■ achieve「成し遂げる」
- tendency「傾向、風潮」 ■ syndrome「症候群（一群の病的な症状）」 ■ the prime minister「首相」
- get rid of「…を取り除く」 ■ be pulled down「引きずり下ろされる」

Comprehension Check — Read the sentences below about the passage. Circle True or False.

1. *Deru kui wa utareru* happens only in Japan. [True / False]
2. The expression "tall poppy" usually has a negative meaning. [True / False]
3. The expression "tall poppy" originally comes from gardening. [True / False]
4. "Tall poppies" are seen as deserving their success. [True / False]
5. John Howard thought "tall poppy syndrome" was a problem in Australia. [True / False]

Your Opinions — Circle the words/phrases in the brackets below to show your opinions. Then, compare your sentences with your partner.

1. I think the proverb *deru kui wa utareru* is [still true / outdated] in Japan now.
2. I [feel / don't feel] envious of those who are more successful than me.
3. Generally speaking, I [respect / don't respect] my country's leaders.

Build a Happy Life!

Astrid Klein

Architect, Klein Dytham architecture

Warm-up | **Look at the unit title and the picture above. Answer the questions below.**

1. What do you think that is next to this woman?
2. Which country's flag is this? What are three things you know about this country?

Key Vocabulary | **Match each word/phrase with the correct meaning.**

[   ] **1.** architect (n.)   **a.** study or learn to do something

[   ] **2.** challenging (adj.)   **b.** saying or showing your feelings or desires directly

[   ] **3.** conservative (adj.)   **c.** share some same points or features

[   ] **4.** have in common (v.)   **d.** new; unique; creative

[   ] **5.** honest (adj.)   **e.** chance or opportunity

[   ] **6.** innovative (adj.)   **f.** a person who designs buildings

[   ] **7.** passionate (adj.)   **g.** safe; traditional; not crazy

[   ] **8.** playful (adj.)   **h.** difficult; takes time to finish or do

[   ] **9.** possibility (n.)   **i.** having strong feelings or desire to do something

[   ] **10.** train (v.)   **j.** fun and interesting

Introduction

   DVD VIDEO · CD2 03

First Viewing **Watch the Introduction. Number the pictures in the order in which they appear.**

a

Astrid went to an international school.

b

Astrid designs many styles of buildings.

c

Astrid works on interior design, too.

d

Astrid has a business partner.

Second Viewing **Watch the Introduction again. Fill in the missing information in Astrid's profile. In [1]–[7], write the correct words from the box. In [a]–[c], write the correct numbers/years.**

Name: _Astrid Klein_   **Birth country:** _____

Job: _architect_   **Nationality:** _____

Background & Career:

- Astrid has been working in Japan for [a.   ] years.
- She's an architect, but she's also trained in [1.   ] [2.   ].
- At an international school, she studied [3.   ] in French, [4.   ] in German, and [5.   ] in Italian.
- She came to Japan with her business partner in [b.   ]. They set up Klein Dytham architecture [c.   ] years later.
- Now they design [6.   ] and [7.   ] buildings.

art
design
history
impressive
interior
math
playful

Interview

Predicting Read the titles of Topics 1–3 below. What do you think each title means? Write your own ideas. Then, compare your ideas with a partner.

Topic 1: Be open to new things.

_____

Topic 2: Challenge is fun.

_____

Topic 3: Be honest with yourself.

_____

T O P I C 1 Be open to new things.

First Viewing Watch Topic 1. Number Astrid's statements in the order in which you hear them.

[   ] It's very hard to design new buildings.
[   ] In Japan you can make things that would be difficult to make in other countries.
[   ] The buildings in Japan were all so wild and crazy.
[   ] Japanese people are very open to new things.

Second Viewing Watch Topic 1 again. Circle True or False.

1. Astrid wanted to come to Japan because of the architecture. [True / False]
2. Europe is more conservative than Japan. [True / False]
3. Buildings in Europe are wild and crazy. [True / False]
4. Japanese buildings use innovative materials. [True / False]
5. Japanese people are afraid of new things. [True / False]

TOPIC 2 Challenge is fun.

First Viewing Watch Topic 2. Number Alice's questions in the order in which you hear them.

[   ] That is fun. What was new?

[   ] In your work, what's important to you?

[   ] That is more than architects usually do. Wasn't it difficult?

[   ] So which of your recent projects was both new and fun?

Second Viewing Watch Topic 2 again. Circle the correct answer to each question.

1. Overall, what kind of work does Astrid like?
   a. Easy but well-paid
   b. Exciting but serious
   c. Challenging but fun

2. How did Astrid feel about designing the Tsutaya bookstore in Daikanyama?
   a. It was very difficult, but she enjoyed the experience.
   b. It was easy because she had designed many buildings before.
   c. It was too difficult, so she doesn't want to do such a big project again.

TOPIC 3 Be honest with yourself.

First Viewing Watch Topic 3. Fill in Astrid's missing words. Write one word in each blank.

1. Only you know what [   ] you [   ].

2. If you like doing something, you'll [   ] [   ] [   ].

3. If you want a happy life, you have to [   ] it [   ].

Second Viewing Watch Topic 3 again. Complete the summary using the words in the box below.

Astrid believes it's important to find work which you [1.   ]. You should be [2.   ] about what you do. Show your [3.   ], and put away your [4.   ]. You have to make a happy [5.   ] yourself, as no one will [6.   ] it for you!

| build | enjoy | life | modesty | passion | passionate |

open to new things

"Open to new things" is another way of saying that you want to try new things and have many experiences.

Work in pairs. Practice this useful expression from the video.

1 Watch how Astrid uses this expression. Then, practice the dialogue below with your partner.

DVD VIDEO   CD2 07

Alice: So you see Japan as a land of possibility?

Astrid: Absolutely. Japanese people are very **open to new things**.

2 Listen to the example dialogue below. Practice it with your partner.

DVD AUDIO   CD2 08

A: I think it's important to be **open to new things**.

B: I agree. I'd like to try scuba diving in the future.

A: Wow, that sounds exciting. Why do you want to try scuba diving?

B: Because I want to explore underwater and see beautiful fish.

3 Fill in the blanks below with your own ideas. Then, practice the completed dialogue with your partner.

A: I think it's important to be **open to new things**.

B: I agree. I'd like to _____ in the future.

A: Wow, that sounds exciting. Why do you want to _____ ?

B: Because _____ .

Sharing Your Ideas   **Finding the Best Job**

What is most important for you when looking for a job? Check (✓) the most important thing below. Also, write one idea of your own. Then, compare your ideas with your partner.

I want to find a job which:
- ☐ has a high salary.
- ☐ has a lot of holidays.
- ☐ has many nice co-workers.
- ☐ is in a good location.
- ☐ is very challenging.
- ☐ is very fun.

your idea: _____ .

Reading Passage

Finally! A Better Way to Make Presentations!

How many times have you listened to a long, boring presentation? Fifty times? A | 01
hundred times? Architects Astrid Klein and Mark Dytham have invented a better | 02
way! It's called "PechaKucha 20 x 20." You probably recognize the first part of that | 03
name, which is Japanese and means "chit chat," or an informal, friendly way of | 04
talking. PechaKucha 20 x 20 is a simple presentation format: you show 20 images, | 05
each for 20 seconds. The images advance automatically and you talk along to the | 06
images. When all the slides have been shown, you're done. There's no stopping and | 07
no going back. Why did Astrid and Mark invent this format? Because architects talk | 08
too much! Give a microphone to a creative person and they'll talk forever. But with | 09
a limit on slides and the auto-advance feature, anyone can give a short, concise | 10
presentation. Astrid and Mark organized the first PechaKucha Night in Tokyo in 2003 | 11
so young designers could meet, network, and show their work to others. The idea | 12
has since spread around the world, and there are PechaKucha Nights in 700 cities. | 13
Anyone can use the format. Astrid's daughter presented when she was five years | 14
old (about her art work). Mark's mother presented when she was 69 (about the fancy | 15
wedding cakes she makes). How could you use PechaKucha 20 x 20? What would you | 16
talk about? [226 words] | 17

Notes ■ invent「発案する」 ■ chit chat「おしゃべり、雑談」 ■ advance「前へ進む」 ■ microphone「マイク」
■ auto-advance feature「自動前進機能」 ■ concise「簡潔な」 ■ fancy「装飾的な」

Comprehension Check **Read the sentences below about the passage. Circle True or False.**

1. According to the passage, presentations are usually exciting to listen to. [True / False]
2. The expression "PechaKucha" comes from the Japanese language. [True / False]
3. In a PechaKucha presentation, you can talk as long as you want. [True / False]
4. PechaKucha was invented because architects talk too much. [True / False]
5. People of all ages can give a PechaKucha presentation. [True / False]

Your Opinions **Circle the words/phrases in the brackets below to show your opinions. Then, compare your sentences with your partner.**

1. In general, I think listening to presentations is [interesting / boring].
2. I think good presentation skills will be [very important / not so important] for my future career.
3. To me, a six-minute and forty-second presentation sounds very [short / long].

Life Is Like Riding a Bicycle

Sachiko Takao
Freelance Designer and Advertising Consultant

Warm-up   **Look at the unit title and the picture above. Answer the questions below.**

1. What do you think this woman designs?
2. This woman did something amazing on her bicycle. What do you think it was?

Key Vocabulary   **Match each word/phrase with the correct meaning.**

[   ] **1.** abroad (adv.)   **a.** pay someone to do a job
[   ] **2.** adventurous (adj.)   **b.** covering all of something
[   ] **3.** advertising (n.)   **c.** something which makes us afraid or scared
[   ] **4.** broadcaster (n.)   **d.** find something new
[   ] **5.** discover (v.)   **e.** finish or complete something difficult
[   ] **6.** employ (v.)   **f.** not found; absent; incomplete
[   ] **7.** fear (n.)   **g.** overseas; in another country
[   ] **8.** get past (v.)   **h.** a person or company which plays television or radio programs
[   ] **9.** missing (adj.)   **i.** planning or designing ways to help someone sell a product
[   ] **10.** whole (adj.)   **j.** wanting to try many exciting or challenging things

Introduction

 DVD VIDEO CD2 11

First Viewing **Watch the Introduction. Number the pictures in the order in which they appear.**

a

Sachi built a successful career in the U.S. and the U.K.

b

Sachi made a bike trip from Okinawa to Hokkaido.

c

Sachi studied at a high school in California for one year.

d

Sachi did internships at major broadcasters.

Second Viewing **Watch the Introduction again. Fill in the missing information in Sachi's profile. In [1]–[7], write the correct words from the box.**

Name: Sachiko Takao   **Hometown:** _____

Job: freelance website designer and online advertising consultant

Background & Career:

- Sachi lives in a "[1.   ] apartment," where

  [2.   ] share living and work spaces.

- Although she's an only [3.   ], her mother encouraged

  her to see the [4.   ].

- She went to university in the U.S. and majored in [5.   ]

  and [6.   ] arts.

- After returning to Japan, she made a bike trip from Okinawa to Hokkaido

  and [7.   ] local Japanese foods to the world.

cinema
daughter
introduced
residents
social
television
world

Interview

Predicting Read the titles of Topics 1–3 below. What do you think each title means? Write your own ideas. Then, compare your ideas with a partner.

Topic 1: Freelancing is flexible.

Topic 2: Being with people is important.

Topic 3: Keep moving!

T O P I C 1 Freelancing is flexible.

First Viewing Watch Topic 1. Number Alice's questions or statements in the order in which you hear them.

[   ] How many people does it take to manage all that?
[   ] Ah, you do everything yourself!
[   ] Is that why you decided to work freelance?
[   ] What kind of projects are you working on now?

Second Viewing Watch Topic 1 again. Circle the correct answer to each question.

1. Sachi works as a freelancer. Who is her main client now?
   a. A store selling Disney goods
   b. A social media website
   c. A manufacturer of bicycle frames

2. Overall, why does Sachi like working freelance?
   a. It's a lot of fun and games.
   b. She also has time to work on her own projects.
   c. She has free time to train for triathlons.

T O P I C **2** Being with people is important.

**First
Viewing**   Watch Topic 2. Number Sachi's statements in the order in which you
hear them.

[   ]   I realized Japan needs fun and interesting ways to learn English.

[   ]   When you're with other people, you feed each other ideas.

[   ]   We can cover all kinds of topics, from music to business.

[   ]   I get great ideas from the people I live with.

**Second
Viewing**   Watch Topic 2 again. Circle True or False.

1. Sachi discovered what she wanted to do next during her cycling trip.   [True / False]
2. Only people overseas read Sachi's cycling blog.   [True / False]
3. Sachi loves English.   [True / False]
4. Sachi wants to make a podcast that is only about cycling.   [True / False]
5. Sachi thinks of all of her ideas by herself.   [True / False]

T O P I C **3** Keep moving!

**First
Viewing**   Watch Topic 3. Fill in Sachi's missing words. Write one word in each
blank.

1. I have [   ], like everyone [   ].

2. It's [   ] when I don't know where I'm going or what I [   ] do.

3. If you keep [   ], you will get [   ] your fears.

**Second
Viewing**   Watch Topic 3 again. Complete the summary using the words in the box
below.

Sachi has had an [1.   ] life and now wants to start her own

[2.   ]. But she's not fearless. She also gets [3.   ]

sometimes. However, she agrees with Einstein that "Life is like [4.   ] a

[5.   ]. To keep your [6.   ], you have to keep moving."

    adventurous   afraid   balance   bicycle   business   riding

on top of that

"On top of that" means in addition to other things. You have many things to do at one time.

Work in pairs. Practice this useful expression from the video.

1 Watch how Sachi uses this expression. Then, practice the dialogue below with your partner.

DVD VIDEO CD2 15

Alice: Ah, you do everything yourself!

Sachi: Yes. And **on top of that**, I go to events, like the IRONMAN World Championship in Hawaii.

2 Listen to the example dialogue below. Then, practice it with your partner.

DVD AUDIO CD2 16

A: A student's life is very busy, isn't it?

B: Yes, I have to go to many classes. **On top of that**, I also have a part-time job.

A: How often do you do that?

B: I have a part-time job at a convenience store about three days a week.

3 Fill in the blanks below with your own ideas. Then, practice the completed dialogue with your partner.

A: A student's life is very busy, isn't it?

B: Yes, I have to go to many classes. **On top of that**, I also _____.

A: How often do you do that?

B: I _____.

Sharing Your Ideas **Exploring Japan**

If you had seven months to travel around Japan, what would you like to explore? Check (✓) what you would like to explore below. Also, write one of your own ideas. Then, compare your ideas with your partner.

If I had seven months to explore Japan, I'd like to see a lot of:

☐ Japanese castles. ☐ temples and shrines.

☐ Japanese gardens. ☐ natural scenery, such as mountains and lakes.

☐ historical sites. ☐ World Heritage sites in Japan.

your idea: _____.

Reading Passage

Internships—A Win-Win Situation

Before we buy a car, we take it for a test drive. Before we buy ice cream, we ask for 01
a sample. What if you could "test drive" a career before you graduated? In many 02
countries, young people do exactly that—they work for a few months, while they 03
are still students, to see if the career is a good fit for them. This is called "doing 04
an internship." When Sachiko Takao was a student in California, she did several 05
internships. She wasn't paid, and she only worked at the companies for a short time, 06
but she learned a lot about how television programs are made. She also learned skills 07
that helped her find a good job after graduation. She even earned university credits 08
for doing the internships! In some cases, internships lead to job offers. That's one of 09
the benefits of internships for employers. By offering internships, they can attract 10
talented students to their companies. And they can "test drive" the students before 11
they offer them a job. It's a win-win situation, in which both students and employers 12
benefit. [180 words] 13

Notes ■ win-win「双方にメリットのある」 ■ a good fit for「…に適合すること」
■ benefit「利益、利益を得る」 ■ talented「有能な、優れた」

Comprehension Check **Read the sentences below about the passage. Circle True or False.**

1. When Sachi did internships in university, she spent a long time doing an internship
   at each company. [True / False]
2. Sachi got paid for the work she did her internships. [True / False]
3. Doing internships helped Sachi find a job after graduation. [True / False]
4. Sachi could get university credit for doing internships. [True / False]
5. Only students benefit from internships. There is no benefit to employers. [True / False]

Your Opinions **Circle the words/phrases in the brackets below to show your opinions. Then, compare your sentences with your partner.**

1. As of now, I think I [have enough / need more] skills to find a good job.
2. I [know / don't know] the type of company I would like to work for after I graduate.
3. I am [interested / not so interested] in doing an internship while I'm a student.
4. I think universities in Japan [should / should not] require all students to do an
   internship.

Trade Ideas for Positive Change

Christopher Faulkner
Business Development Manager,
Mitsui & Co., Ltd.

Warm-up

Look at the unit title and the picture. Answer the questions below.

1. What kind of job do you think this man has?
2. Which country's flag is this? What are three things you know about this country?

Key Vocabulary

Match each word/phrase with the correct meaning.

[ ] **1.** accomplish (v.)   **a.** think of an idea or solution

[ ] **2.** benefit (n.)   **b.** very important; needs to be taken care of right now

[ ] **3.** capture (v.)   **c.** what you get from studying something new

[ ] **4.** come up with (v.)   **d.** make something smaller or less

[ ] **5.** fuel (n.)   **e.** finish something and cause a successful result

[ ] **6.** knowledge (n.)   **f.** having connections with several different countries

[ ] **7.** multinational (adj.) **g.** an energy source for engines or power plants

[ ] **8.** reduce (v.)   **h.** bonus; reward; good point

[ ] **9.** resource (n.)   **i.** supply; support; aid

[ ] **10.** urgent (adj.)   **j.** catch; get

Introduction

DVD VIDEO   CD2 19

First Viewing **Watch the Introduction. Number the pictures in the order in which they appear.**

Chris traveled around Europe.

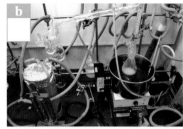

Chris did research in a science lab.

Chris received a certificate for studying Japanese.

Chris was good at science when he was young.

Second Viewing **Watch the Introduction again. Fill in the missing information in Chris's profile. In [1]–[8], write the correct words from the box. In [a], write the correct number.**

Name: Christopher Faulkner   **Home country:** _____

Job: business development manager

Background & Career:

- Chris works on innovative [1.   ] projects.
- He was born and [2.   ] in Australia and started studying Japanese there when he was [a.   ] years old.
- He dreamed of using [3.   ] to make the world a better place.
- Before starting university, he [4.   ] around Europe.
- In university he earned a [5.   ] degree in [6.   ] and [7.   ].
- He did his [8.   ] degree at Tokyo University.

backpacked
double
energy
engineering
Japanese
master's
raised
science

Interview

Predicting Read the titles of Topics 1–3 below. What do you think each title means? Write your own ideas. Then, compare your ideas with a partner.

Topic 1: A big company offers big possibilities.

Topic 2: Put your knowledge to work.

Topic 3: Change the world with the power of many.

T O P I C 1 A big company offers big possibilities.

First Viewing Watch Topic 1. Number Chris's statements in the order in which you hear them.

[   ] I knew I wanted to work globally.
[   ] A big company offers big possibilities.
[   ] The impossible becomes possible.
[   ] I saw a lot of room for growth for me personally.

Second Viewing Watch Topic 1 again. Circle True or False.

1. Chris wanted to work for a smaller company. [True / False]
2. Chris is a very active worker. [True / False]
3. Chris joined a multinational company so he could enjoy traveling. [True / False]
4. Chris has worked only in Japan. [True / False]
5. Combining workers from different countries is good for a company. [True / False]

T O P I C **2** Put your knowledge to work.

First Viewing Watch Topic 2. Number Alice's questions or statements in the order in which you hear them.

[   ] These are urgent needs, aren't they?

[   ] And energy in liquid form is relatively easy to transport and trade.

[   ] That sounds like a double benefit.

[   ] Are you using that knowledge now in your job?

Second Viewing Watch Topic 2 again. Circle the correct answer to each question.

1. How is Chris using the research he did at Tokyo University in his current job?

a. He is working on a project which makes nuclear power safer.

b. He is working on a project which will make gas for cars cheaper.

c. He is working on a project to make cheap and clean energy.

2. What is Chris's opinion about the future of energy?

a. It will be impossible to reduce CO_2 emissions.

b. Today's students will find new solutions.

c. Energy will become more expensive for all countries.

T O P I C **3** Change the world with the power of many.

First Viewing Watch Topic 3. Fill in Chris's missing words. Write one word in each blank.

1. So I looked for a job where I could [   ] [   ] with others.

2. Aristotle said, "The [   ] is greater than the sum of its [   ]."

3. With the power of [   ], it *is* possible to [   ] the [   ].

Second Viewing Watch Topic 3 again. Complete the summary using the words in the box below.

Since Chris didn't [1.   ] to work [2.   ], he looked for a job where he could work with [3.   ]. After all, you can [4.   ] more when working with many [5.   ]. It's possible to make a [6.   ] world if lots of people get [7.   ].

| accomplish | alone | better | others | people | together | want |

follow your passion

"Follow your passion" means to do the thing you really love to do in life and try to make it your career.

Work in pairs. Practice this useful expression from the video.

1 Watch how Alice uses this expression. Then, practice the statement below with your partner.

DVD VIDEO · CD2 23

Alice: When students are thinking about their future careers, everyone tells them to **follow their passion**.

2 Listen to the example dialogue below. Then, practice it with your partner.

DVD AUDIO · CD2 24

A: They say you should **follow your passion** in life. So, can you tell me your passion?

B: My passion is <u>medicine</u>, so my dream is to <u>become a great doctor</u>.

A: That's a great dream. Good luck!

B: Thanks. I'll **follow my passion**!

3 Fill in the blanks below with your own ideas. Then, practice the completed dialogue with your partner.

A: They say you should **follow your passion** in life. So, can you tell me your passion?

B: My passion is _____, so my dream is to _____.

A: That's a great dream. Good luck!

B: Thanks. I'll **follow my passion**!

Sharing Your Ideas · Being Environmentally-Friendly

What can you do in your daily life to be environmentally-friendly? Check (✓) the action that would be easiest for you to do. Also, write one of your own ideas. Then, compare your ideas with your partner.

To be more environmentally-friendly, I think I can:

☐ recycle all my garbage carefully.   ☐ reuse shopping bags or use a *furoshiki*.

☐ take a shower instead of a bath.   ☐ use less hot water.

☐ cut down on using the air conditioner and heater.

☐ use public transportation instead of driving my own car.

your idea: _____.

Reading Passage

Gaps Can Be Good: The Advantages of a Gap Year

In Japan, any gap in your academic or working career is generally seen as a problem. 01
Words like *ronin* (studying independently to retake university entrance exams), 02
kyugaku (taking a leave of absence from school) and *ryunen* (repeating a year) all 03
have negative connotations. Yet in most English-speaking countries, including the 04
United States, Australia and Canada, many students don't study "straight through" 05
to finish university in three or four years. Instead, they take time off to do other 06
things. For example, Christopher Faulkner, who is introduced in this unit, took a 07
gap year after high school to backpack around Europe. During university, he took off 08
another year to go to Japan and learn Japanese. What sort of things do other students 09
do during their gap years? Many travel abroad. Others do volunteer work, or learn a 10
foreign language or other special skill. Even the British crown princes, William and 11
Harry, took gap years. Prince William traveled to Australia, Argentina and Africa 12
during his gap year, and made a documentary film about orphans in Lesotho. Prince 13
Harry did volunteer work in Chile during his gap year. In many countries, a gap year 14
is seen as a positive use of time. It is seen as a way to gain experience that will be 15
useful when you return to your studies, or later in life. Do you think "gap years" will 16
ever become accepted in Japan? What could you do if you could take a year off from 17
university? [245 words] 18

Notes
■ independently「独立して」 ■ a leave of absence「休暇」 ■ connotation「言外の意味」 ■ yet「けれども」
■ crown「王権」 ■ orphan「孤児」 ■ Lesotho「レソト (アフリカ南部に位置する王政国家)」
■ Chile「チリ (南米南西部に位置する共和国)」

Comprehension Check **Read the sentences below about the passage. Circle True or False.**

1. Gaps in your career in Japan are usually seen as OK. [True / False]
2. Taking time off from studying is normal in most English-speaking countries.
   [True / False]
3. Christopher Faulkner took two gap years during his studies. [True / False]
4. When taking a gap year, most students just relax and have fun. [True / False]

Your Opinions **Circle the words/phrases in the brackets below to show your opinions. Then, compare your sentences with your partner.**

1. After reading this passage, I now have a [positive / negative] image about gap years.
2. In the future, I think that gap years [will / won't] become more accepted in Japan.
3. I [would / would not] like to take a gap year during university.

Unit 11

Connect Workers With Companies

Annie Chang
President, AC Global Solutions Ltd.

Warm-up Look at the unit title and the picture above. Answer the questions below.

1. Why do you think this woman has so many computers and smart phones?
2. Which country's flag is this? What are three things you know about this country?

| **Key Vocabulary** | Match each word with the correct meaning. | |

[   ] **1.** ambitious (adj.)   **a.** look for new people to join a team or company

[   ] **2.** application (n.)   **b.** a person who is trying to get a job or other position

[   ] **3.** attitude (n.)   **c.** feeling that you are good at something or can do it

[   ] **4.** candidate (n.)   **d.** something which has a special use or purpose

[   ] **5.** comfort (n.)   **e.** related to money or banking

[   ] **6.** compete (v.)   **f.** wanting to be successful; having big dreams

[   ] **7.** confident (adj.)   **g.** feeling of being relaxed or used to a situation

[   ] **8.** financial (adj.)   **h.** technique for doing something

[   ] **9.** method (n.)   **i.** trying to get something; trying to be better than others

[   ] **10.** recruit (v.)   **j.** feeling or manner about someone or something

Introduction

First Viewing

Watch the Introduction. Number the pictures in the order in which they appear.

Annie has appeared in magazines and newspapers.

Annie was a high school teacher.

Annie sometimes interviews others.

Annie didn't have a job when she came to Japan.

Second Viewing

Watch the Introduction again. Fill in the missing information in Annie's profile. In [1]–[7], write the correct words from the box. In [a] and [b], write the correct years.

Name: _Annie Chang_   **Home country:** _____

Job: _president_

Background & Career:

- As president of an IT [1. _____] company, Annie looks for workers with good [2. _____] skills.

- She came to Japan in [a. _____], but didn't speak [3. _____].

- She learned [4. _____] while working in a computer store.

- In [b. _____], she started her own company.

- Because IT recruiting was [5. _____] in Japan at that time, she is considered a [6. _____].

- By coming to Japan, she could discover her [7. _____].

> computer
> English
> Japanese
> pioneer
> recruiting
> strengths
> unusual

Interview

Predicting Read the titles of Topics 1–3 below. What do you think each title means? Write your own ideas. Then, compare your ideas with a partner.

Topic 1: Get out of your comfort zone.

_____

Topic 2: If you try, people will help you.

_____

Topic 3: Try this method for relaxed interviews.

_____

T O P I C 1 Get out of your comfort zone.

First Viewing Watch Topic 1. Number Alice's questions in the order in which you hear them.

[　]　So, what's the solution?
[　]　Can young Japanese compete?
[　]　What are these companies looking for?
[　]　Where do you find workers with good technical skills?

Second Viewing Watch Topic 1 again. Circle True or False.

1. All of Annie's clients are Japanese.   [True / False]
2. Companies are especially looking for people with technical skills. [True / False]
3. Programmers from many foreign companies are coming to Japan.   [True / False]
4. According to Annie, young Japanese are very ambitious.   [True / False]
5. It is important for young Japanese to try more challenging things. [True / False]

T O P I C **2** If you try, people will help you.   DVD VIDEO   CD2 29

First Viewing Watch Topic 2. Number Annie's statements in the order in which you hear them.

[ ] Companies need staff who can communicate with people from all over the world.

[ ] The desire to communicate is more important than how well you speak.

[ ] All companies want people with a positive attitude.

[ ] These days, companies are operating all over the globe.

Second Viewing Watch Topic 2 again. Circle the correct answer to each question.

1. According to Annie, what is the most important thing for candidates?

  a. Experience

  b. English skills

  c. Attitude

2. What is Annie's main piece of advice in this interview?

  a. If you travel to many countries, you can succeed.

  b. If you master many skills, you can succeed.

  c. If you have ambition and desire, you can succeed.

T O P I C **3** Try this method for relaxed interviews.   DVD VIDEO   CD2 30

First Viewing Watch Topic 3. Fill in Annie's missing words. Write one word in each blank.

1. That makes you [   ] confident and [   ] confident.

2. A smile [   ] you. And it [   ] the other person, too.

3. I tell my [   ] to practice...with a [   ].

Second Viewing Watch Topic 3 again. Complete the summary using the words in the box below.

It's natural to get [¹·   ] during interviews, but Annie has some great

[²·   ] to help you. She says it's important to smile and make eye

[³·   ]. Although it might not be [⁴·   ] for Japanese people,

anyone can get [⁵·   ] to it. It just takes [⁶·   ]!

contact   easy   methods   nervous   practice   used

look for ... in

"Look for ... in" means to hope to find certain features or traits in someone or something.

Work in pairs. Practice this useful expression from the video.

1 Watch how Alice uses this expression. Then, practice the dialogue below with your partner.

DVD VIDEO CD2 31

Alice: What are companies really **looking for in** a candidate?

Annie: The number one thing is attitude.

2 Listen to the example dialogue below. Then, practice it with your partner.

DVD AUDIO CD2 32

A: What do you **look for in** a friend?

B: Hmmm, I want a friend who has a good sense of humor.

A: Why is that so important?

B: Because when I'm with my friends I want to have fun and relax.

3 Fill in the blanks below with your own ideas. Then, practice the completed dialogue with your partner.

A: What do you **look for in** a friend?

B: Hmmm, I want a friend who _____.

A: Why is that so important?

B: Because _____.

Sharing Your Ideas **Competing in the Job Market**

It's very challenging to compete in the global employment market. What do you think your own best skill or trait is? Check (✓) your strongest point below. Also, write one of your own ideas. Then, compare your ideas with your partner.

I think my strongest skill or trait for the job market is my:
☐ attitude.
☐ communication skills.
☐ computer skills.
☐ foreign language skills.
☐ presentation skills.

your idea: _____.

Reading Passage

What Does "IT" Really Mean?

You've probably heard the term "IT" (pronounced "eye-tee") but do you know what   01
it really means? If someone asked you, could you tell them what the two letters   02
stand for? Actually, "IT" is an abbreviation for "information technology." It may   03
seem like a recent term, but in fact it's over 50 years old. It first appeared in 1958 in   04
an article in the *Harvard Business Review*, a famous magazine for business studies.   05
Information technology is the branch of engineering that uses computers and   06
telecommunications to collect, send and store information. IT jobs include computer   07
programming, network administration, computer engineering, Web development,   08
technical support, and many other related occupations. Many companies now have   09
IT departments that manage the computers, networks, and other technical areas of   10
their businesses. Most people don't realize it, but IT is a big part of our daily lives. For   11
example, did you play a game on your phone today? Did you use a smart card to pay   12
for a bus ride? Did you get cash from an ATM? All of these systems use information   13
technology. Try to think of other examples in your own daily life. Once you start   14
looking for IT, you'll realize it's everywhere. It's no exaggeration when people say we   15
live in the "information age."   [211 words]   16

Notes ■ stand for「…を表す」 ■ abbreviation「略語」 ■ telecommunication「遠隔通信」
■ network administration「ネットワーク管理」 ■ occupation「職業」 ■ exaggeration「誇張表現」

Comprehension Check Read the sentences below about the passage. Circle True or False.

1. "IT" is a recent term.   [True / False]
2. The term "IT" first appeared in an engineering journal.   [True / False]
3. IT departments are now a part of many companies.   [True / False]
4. IT has many uses in our daily lives.   [True / False]
5. IT jobs usually mean only computer programmers.   [True / False]

Your Opinions Circle the words/phrases in the brackets below to show your opinions. Then, compare your sentences with your partner.

1. Before reading this passage, I [knew / didn't know] what "IT" stands for.
2. At this point, I feel my own computer skills are [strong / average / weak].
3. I think computer skills will be [very important / not so important] for my future job.
4. Before reading this passage, I [already realized / didn't yet realize] how important IT is in daily life.

12

Necessity Is the Mother of Invention

Sreekumar Bhanuvikraman Pillai Ambika

Chief Technology Officer, EP Consulting Services

Look at the unit title and the picture. Answer the questions below.

1. What kind of job do you think this man has?
2. Which country's flag is this? What are three things you know about this country?

Key Vocabulary   Match each word/phrase with the correct meaning.

 DVD AUDIO CD2 34

[　]	**1.** adjust (v.)	**a.** hardworking; active; ambitious
[　]	**2.** develop (v.)	**b.** not a good use of something; meaningless
[　]	**3.** device (n.)	**c.** not active; doesn't try new things
[　]	**4.** enterprising (adj.)	**d.** look for; try to find
[　]	**5.** invention (n.)	**e.** a machine or tool
[　]	**6.** necessity (n.)	**f.** chance or space for something new
[　]	**7.** passive (adj.)	**g.** change to try to fit a new situation
[　]	**8.** room (n.)	**h.** make or create something new
[　]	**9.** seek out (v.)	**i.** something which we need in our lives
[　]	**10.** waste (n.)	**j.** a new creation or product

Introduction

First Viewing — **Watch the Introduction. Number the pictures in the order in which they appear.**

Sreekumar came to Japan from India.

Sreekumar's family didn't have enough money for a computer.

Sreekumar manages an international team.

Sreekumar is an enterprising IT engineer.

Second Viewing — **Watch the Introduction again. Fill in the missing information in Sreekumar's profile. In [1]–[7], write the correct words from the box. In [a], write the correct year.**

Name: Sreekumar Bhanuvikraman Pillai Ambika   **Home country:** _____

Job: chief technology officer _____

Background & Career:

- Sreekumar manages a team of [1.   ] and
  [2.   ] who help other companies with IT solutions.
- He came to Japan in [a.   ] after studying [3.   ]
  at one of the best [4.   ] in India.
- Since high school, he planned to have a [5.   ] in IT.
- Although his family couldn't [6.   ] a computer,
  a local business owner bought him one. So, he promised to write
  computer [7.   ] to help with the man's business.

> afford
> career
> engineering
> engineers
> programmers
> programs
> universities

Interview

Predicting Read the titles of Topics 1–3 below. What do you think each title means? Write your own ideas. Then, compare your ideas with a partner.

Topic 1: There's always room to innovate.

_____

Topic 2: Technology brings people together.

_____

Topic 3: Take initiative.

_____

T O P I C 1 There's always room to innovate.

First Viewing Watch Topic 1. Number Alice's questions or statements in the order in which you hear them.

[   ] So, you turned it into a product.

[   ] Does that mean you're not programming anymore?

[   ] You saw a need, and you developed a solution.

[   ] Oh, that's very convenient.

Second Viewing Watch Topic 1 again. Circle the correct answer to each question.

1. At his company, what kind of work does Sreekumar mainly do now?

   a. He is only a manager.

   b. He only does programming.

   c. He's a manager, but he still programs, too.

2. What is Sreekumar's feeling about work?

   a. We can always change and make things better.

   b. If things are good now, we don't need to change them.

   c. We should care only about our own company.

T O P I C 2 **Technology brings people together.**

Watch Topic 2. Number Sreekumar's statements in the order in which you hear them.

[ ] Technology has the power to bring people together.

[ ] There wasn't even a website for the Indian community.

[ ] The weather was cold and I wasn't used to the food.

[ ] The website was a catalyst for the community to become more active.

Watch Topic 2 again. Circle True or False.

1. Sreekumar could speak Japanese well when he first came to Japan.   [True / False]
2. Sreekumar created a website for the Indian community.   [True / False]
3. Sreekumar helps to organize many events to share Indian culture.   [True / False]
4. Only Indian people can go to Indian movie nights.   [True / False]
5. Indian movies have a lot of music.   [True / False]

T O P I C 3 **Take initiative.**

Watch Topic 3. Fill in Sreekumar's missing words. Write one word in each blank.

1. It's a waste to use technology just for [   ] and [   ].

2. Think about how you can [   ] technology in [   ]

   [   ].

3. Don't be [   ]; take initiative.

Watch Topic 3 again. Complete the summary using the words in the box below.

Smart [1.   ] and smart [2.   ] are not only for fun. They are actually very powerful [3.   ]. So, you should think about how the [4.   ] company knows if you have [5.   ] on your card. Think about the importance of [6.   ] in your life.

| cards | devices | money | phones | technology | train |

be/get used to

"Be/Get used to" something means that we adjust to something new or come to like it.

Work in pairs. Practice this useful expression from the video.

1 Watch how Sreekumar uses this expression. Then, practice the dialogue below with your partner.

DVD VIDEO | CD2 39

Alice: Did you have trouble adjusting to life in a new country?

Sreekumar: At first I was a little homesick. The weather was cold and I **wasn't used to** the food.

2 Listen to the example dialogue below. Then, practice it with your partner.

DVD AUDIO | CD2 40

A: What do you think would be the most difficult thing to **get used to** in a new country?

B: I think it would be difficult to **get used to** driving.

A: Why would that be so difficult to **get used to**?

B: Driving would be difficult to **get used to** because there are different driving rules in each country. I'm afraid to get in an accident.

3 Fill in the blanks below with your own ideas. Then, practice the completed dialogue with your partner.

A: What do you think would be the most difficult thing to **get used to** in a new country?

B: I think it would be difficult to **get used to** _____.

A: Why would that be so difficult to **get used to**?

B: _____ would be difficult to **get used to** because _____

_____.

Sharing Your Ideas   Using Technology in Your Daily Life

What do you think is the most important way to use technology such as computers and smart phones? Check (✓) the most important way below. Also, write one of your own ideas. Then, compare your ideas with your partner.

The most important way to use technology in my daily life is to:

☐ communicate with family and friends.   ☐ study a foreign language.

☐ study and do research for university classes.   ☐ play games.

your idea: _____.

Reading Passage

Escape to India—Through Movies!

You've certainly seen Hollywood movies but have you ever seen a Bollywood movie? 01
"Bollywood" is the nickname for the cinema industry in Mumbai, the largest city in 02
India, and a combination of "Bombay" (the old name for Mumbai) and "Hollywood." 03
The first movie made in India was a silent film released in 1912, and ever since, 04
movies have been big business there. In fact, more films are made in India than 05
anywhere else in the world. Bollywood movies are a lot of fun, featuring huge casts, 06
colorful costumes and lots of singing and dancing. The music is fantastic, usually 07
a catchy mix of traditional Indian instruments and modern hip hop. Sometimes 08
you hear parodies of popular songs like "The Macarena" or rapping in the Hindi 09
language. The dance scenes, in particular, are amazing: in one movie, hundreds 10
of people danced in perfect unison on top of a moving train! Bollywood movies 11
are usually in Hindi, which is the fourth-most spoken language in the world, and 12
only rarely have English subtitles. But it's easy to follow the story even if you don't 13
understand the words. The plots are always about familiar themes—love, jealousy 14
and revenge! Bollywood movies are the perfect way to escape everyday life—and 15
learn about India and Indian culture. [212 words] 16

Notes
- Mumbai「ムンバイ（インド西岸に位置する大都市）」 ■ silent film「無声映画」 ■ feature「…を特徴にする」
- instrument「楽器」 ■ Hindi「ヒンディー語（インドの公用語の一つ）」 ■ in particular「特に」
- in perfect unison「完全に一致して」 ■ rarely「めったに…しない」 ■ plot「話の筋」 ■ revenge「復讐」

Comprehension Check **Read the sentences below about the passage. Circle True or False.**

1. Bombay is the name of a city in India now. [True / False]
2. The first Indian movie had a lot of music. [True / False]
3. More movies are made in India than any other country in the world. [True / False]
4. In Bollywood movies, you can hear both traditional and modern music. [True / False]
5. Most Bollywood movies have English subtitles. [True / False]

Your Opinions **Circle the words/phrases in the brackets below to show your opinions. Then, compare your sentences with your partner.**

1. I [have / have never] seen a Bollywood movie.
2. Before reading this passage, I [knew / didn't know] that more movies are made in Bollywood than Hollywood.
3. I [like / don't like] movies with a lot of singing and dancing.
4. I think it's better to watch foreign movies [with / without] subtitles.

13

What's the Recipe for Success?

Philippe Batton

Chef and Owner, Le Petit Tonneau

Warm-up | Look at the unit title and the picture above.
Answer the questions below.

1. What kind of food do you think this man serves in his restaurants?
2. Which country's flag is this? What are three things you know about this country?

Key Vocabulary | Match each word/phrase with the correct meaning.

 DVD AUDIO CD2 42

[ ]	**1.** affordable (adj.)	**a.** do something poorly; not succeed or pass
[ ]	**2.** collaborate (v.)	**b.** the different foods we put in a dish when cooking
[ ]	**3.** cuisine (n.)	**c.** a style of cooking, such as Japanese, Italian, French, etc.
[ ]	**4.** fail (v.)	**d.** try to make more people know about something
[ ]	**5.** ingredients (n.)	**e.** work together with others on some project or event
[ ]	**6.** out of reach (ph.)	**f.** reasonably priced; not too expensive
[ ]	**7.** promote (v.)	**g.** famous; many people know this person or place
[ ]	**8.** tool (n.)	**h.** too far, difficult, or expensive
[ ]	**9.** well-known (adj.)	**i.** go to a higher and higher position at one's job
[ ]	**10.** work one's way up (v.)	**j.** things we use to do some job, such as a knife for cooking

Introduction

DVD VIDEO   CD2 43

> **First Viewing**

Watch the Introduction. Number the pictures in the order in which they appear.

Philippe appears at many events.

Philippe worked at one of the best hotels in Paris.

The French government has honored Philippe.

Philippe spent a year in Kobe.

> **Second Viewing**

Watch the Introduction again. Fill in the missing information in Philippe's profile. In [1]–[7], write the correct words from the box. In [a]–[c], write the correct numbers/years.

Name: *Philippe Batton*   **Home country:** _____

Job: *chef and restaurant owner*

Background & Career:

- Philippe owns two [¹·   ] French restaurants in Tokyo.

  They are [²·   ] bistros with [³·   ] food.

- He started his [⁴·   ] when he was only [ᵃ·   ] years

  old and [⁵·   ] his way up to the kitchen at a hotel in Paris.

- After spending a year in Kobe in [ᵇ·   ], he moved back to Japan

  [ᶜ·   ] years later.

- He also [⁶·   ] French food and wine and

  [⁷·   ] cookbooks.

affordable
casual
popular
publishes
promotes
training
worked

Interview

Predicting **Read the titles of Topics 1–3 below. What do you think each title means? Write your own ideas. Then, compare your ideas with a partner.**

Topic 1: Go for it!

_____

Topic 2: If you don't give, you don't get.

_____

Topic 3: Life is like a chessboard.

_____

T O P I C 1 Go for it!

First Viewing ▸ **Watch Topic 1. Number Philippe's statements in the order in which you hear them.**

[   ] I didn't like that French food was so expensive.
[   ] I saw a niche in the market.
[   ] There are always risks when you do something new.
[   ] I was in the right place at the right time.

Second Viewing ▸ **Watch Topic 1 again. Circle True or False.**

1. Philippe came to Japan for the first time when he was a teenager.   [True / False]
2. Philippe thinks Japanese chefs are very good at cooking.   [True / False]
3. Philippe thought French food in Japan was too expensive.   [True / False]
4. Philippe saw many "bistro" when he first came to Japan.   [True / False]
5. Philippe is afraid to try new things.   [True / False]

TOPIC 2 If you don't give, you don't get.

First Viewing Watch Topic 2. Number Alice's questions or statements in the order in which you hear them.

[   ] So helping others is one part of your recipe for success.
[   ] How, specifically, do you do that?
[   ] You really seem to enjoy being with people.
[   ] And that's your mission? To share French culture with Japan?

Second Viewing Watch Topic 2 again. Circle the correct answer to each question.

1. What kind of work schedule does Philippe have?
   a. He is only cooking in his restaurants every day.
   b. He is busy training his staff and managing his restaurants.
   c. He cooks every day and also attends many events.

2. How does Philippe feel about working with other people?
   a. He's too busy cooking to go out and meet other people.
   b. He thinks you should collaborate with others as much as possible.
   c. He's only interested in collaborating with other chefs.

TOPIC 3 Life is like a chessboard.

First Viewing Watch Topic 3. Fill in Philippe's missing words. Write one word in each blank.

1. Yes, but it hasn't [   ] been [   ].
2. I'm always at [   ] when everyone else is [   ].
3. There's always a [   ] to move [   ].

Second Viewing Watch Topic 3 again. Complete the summary using the words in the box below.

To become a [1.   ] and [2.   ] chef, Philippe had to work very
[3.   ]. Still, sometimes he [4.   ]. Just like in chess, sometimes
you [5.   ] on a black square. Even then, however, there are white squares all
[6.   ] you.

> around   fails   hard   land   successful   well-known

focus on

"Focus on" means to especially work on or put time or effort into one thing.

Work in pairs. Practice this useful expression from the video.

1 Watch how Alice uses this expression. Then, practice the dialogue below with your partner.

DVD VIDEO CD2 47

Alice: Wouldn't it be better to **focus on** your own restaurants?

Philippe: I do focus. I cook and I am in my restaurants every day.

2 Listen to the example dialogue below. Then, practice it with your partner.

DVD AUDIO CD2 48

A: What do you **focus on** in school?

B: I **focus on** studying.

A: Why do you **focus on** that?

B: I **focus on** studying because I have only one chance to be a university student. So, I want to study and learn many things during these four years.

3 Fill in the blanks below with your own ideas. Then, practice the completed dialogue with your partner.

A: What do you **focus on** in school?

B: I **focus on** _____.

A: Why do you **focus on** that?

B: I **focus on** _____ because _____
_____.

Sharing Your Ideas **Promoting Your Own Culture**

Imagine you had the chance to promote Japanese culture in a foreign country. Check (✓) what you would most like to teach about your own culture. Also, write one of your own ideas. Then, compare your ideas with your partner.

If I had the chance to promote Japanese culture in a foreign country, I would like to teach:

☐ the Japanese language. ☐ how to cook Japanese cuisine.

☐ a traditional Japanese martial art, such as kendo or karate.

☐ a traditional Japanese activity, such as the tea ceremony.

your idea: _____.

Reading Passage

Why Is French Food So Good?

French food is known as one of the great cuisines of the world. But what makes it | 01
so good? According to Philippe Batton, a leading French chef in Japan, it's because | 02
France is located right in the middle of Europe. Throughout history, France was | 03
invaded again and again. Each time, the invaders brought new foods and cooking | 04
techniques to France. New ideas and ingredients came in times of peace, too. For | 05
example, when the Italian noblewoman Catherine de Medici came to France to | 06
marry the French king Henry II, she brought her own pastry and ice cream chefs | 07
from Italy. This greatly advanced the art of cooking in France. Over the centuries, the | 08
people of France took the best of each culture and made it part of their own. French | 09
food was also influenced by Japan. In the 1960s, many famous French chefs visited | 10
Japan and took home new ideas, such as smaller portions and an emphasis on light | 11
tastes and beautiful presentation. This became the so-called Nouvelle Cuisine ("new | 12
cuisine") that swept the world in the 1970s. In short, France's reputation for fine food | 13
is not so much based on long-held traditions but on constant change. French food is | 14
good because French cooks and their customers are always open to new ideas. That's | 15
food for thought! [217 words] | 16

Notes
- throughout history「歴史を通じて」 ■ invade「侵略する」 ■ noblewoman「高貴な家柄の女性；貴族の女性」
- art「技術」 ■ portion「一人分の量」 ■ presentation「盛り付け」 ■ sweep the world「世界中に広まる」
- reputation「名声」 ■ fine「上質の」 ■ not so much 〜 but「〜ではなくむしろ…」
- long-held「長年抱き続けてきた」 ■ food for thought「思考の糧、考慮すべきもの」

Comprehension Check → **Read the sentences below about the passage. Circle True or False.**

1. Philippe thinks France's location is one reason its food is so good. [True / False]
2. When France was invaded by other countries, new foods and cooking techniques
   were introduced. [True / False]
3. Over the years, French food has been influenced by many other cultures. [True / False]
4. French chefs thought portion sizes in Japan were too small. [True / False]
5. French cooks think you should just always follow old traditions. [True / False]

Your Opinions → **Circle the words/phrases in the brackets below to show your opinions. Then, compare your sentences with your partner.**

1. I [have / have never] eaten French food.
2. Before reading this passage, I [already knew / had no idea] why French food is so good.
3. When eating at a restaurant, I prefer [smaller / bigger] portions.
4. I think it's best for Japanese cuisine to [change / stay the same].

Help Animals for a Better Society

Elizabeth Oliver
Chair, Animal Refuge Kansai

| **Warm-up** | Look at the unit title and the picture above. Answer the questions below. |

1. This woman works with animals. What kind of job do you think she does?
2. Which country's flag is this? What are three things you know about this country?

| **Key Vocabulary** | Match each word/phrase with the correct meaning. | |

[   ]   **1.** achieve (v.)

[   ]   **2.** care for (v.)

[   ]   **3.** cause (n.)

[   ]   **4.** charitable (adj.)

[   ]   **5.** disaster (n.)

[   ]   **6.** handle (v.)

[   ]   **7.** injured (adj.)

[   ]   **8.** shelter (n.)

[   ]   **9.** take in (v.)

[   ]   **10.** welfare (n.)

a. a terrible event, such as an earthquake, flood, or plane crash

b. hurt; the body is in bad condition because of some accident

c. give a new home to people or animals to help them

d. situation of having health and happiness

e. manage something

f. accomplish; succeed; finish something

g. watch over a person or animal; make sure that they are OK

h. a building used for homeless people or animals to stay in

i. situation we want to support or make better

j. helping others without getting paid for it

Introduction

 DVD VIDEO   CD2 51

First Viewing **Watch the Introduction. Number the pictures in the order in which they appear.**

a

ARK has the most modern animal shelter in Japan.

b

Elizabeth was given an award.

c

Elizabeth grew up with pets.

d

Elizabeth has lived in Kansai for many years.

Second Viewing **Watch the Introduction again. Fill in the missing information in Elizabeth's profile. In [1]–[7], write the correct words from the box. In [a] and [b], write the correct numbers/years.**

Name: Elizabeth Oliver   **Home country:** _____

Job: chair (of Animal Refuge Kansai, ARK, or an NPO) _____

Background & Career:

- Elizabeth is the chair and founder of ARK, an NPO which cares for
  [1.   ] pets and tries to find them new [2.   ].

- She grew up with dogs, cats, and even a [3.   ]!

- As a child, she was taught [4.   ] towards animals.

- She came to Kansai when she was [a.   ] and has now been in
  Kansai for [5.   ] half a [6.   ].

- She founded ARK in [b.   ]. Since then, she and her supporters have
  [7.   ] thousands of animals.

century
homeless
homes
nearly
pony
responsibility
rescued

 **Interview**

Predicting **Read the titles of Topics 1–3 below. What do you think each title means? Write your own ideas. Then, compare your ideas with a partner.**

Topic 1: Find a cause to work for.

Topic 2: There's always a solution.

Topic 3: Don't bite off too much.

T O P I C 1 Find a cause to work for. ● DVD VIDEO CD2 52

First Viewing **Watch Topic 1. Number Alice's questions or statements in the order in which you hear them.**

[   ] What got you interested in animal rescue in the first place?

[   ] That's a nice way to give back to Japan.

[   ] In that time, how many animals have you rescued?

[   ] In Western countries, there are shelters that will take in pets when their owners can't keep them.

Second Viewing **Watch Topic 1 again. Circle True or False.**

1. ARK only cares for dogs. [True / False]
2. ARK built a new facility because they need more space. [True / False]
3. Before creating ARK, Elizabeth felt Japan already had a good system for helping animals.
   [True / False]
4. In Western countries, there are many shelters that will take in pets. [True / False]
5. According to Elizabeth, everyone can contribute to society. [True / False]

T O P I C 2 There's always a solution.

First Viewing Watch Topic 2. Number Elizabeth's statements in the order in which you hear them.

[   ] I now think we need emergency shelters where people can stay with their pets.

[   ] There's always a solution, if you're willing to try something different.

[   ] It was really difficult. But a lot of people came to help.

[   ] So many people lost their homes and couldn't take care of their pets.

Second Viewing Watch Topic 2 again. Circle the correct answer to each question.

1. How did ARK handle so many animals at once after the Kobe earthquake?

    a. They built a new shelter.

    b. They sent animals to England.

    c. A lot of people came to help.

2. What does Elizabeth think is needed to prepare for another disaster in Japan?

    a. Emergency shelters where people and their pets can stay together.

    b. Media coverage to bring in thousands of new volunteers.

    c. Groups of *bosozoku* who are willing to take in homeless pets.

T O P I C 3 Don't bite off too much.

First Viewing Watch Topic 3. Fill in Elizabeth's missing words. Write one word in each blank.

1. If you [   ] [   ] more than you can chew, you won't accomplish

    [   ].

2. Don't start a new project until you have [   ] what you already [   ].

3. If you [   ], you will [   ].

Second Viewing Watch Topic 3 again. Complete the summary using the words in the box below.

Elizabeth says that no one can do [1.   ]. So, her advice is to [2.   ]
what you can [3.   ] get [4.   ] and then [5.   ] it. First,
you should [6.   ] one project. Then, you can [7.   ] on a new one.

actually	decide	do	done	everything	finish	start

in the first place

"In the first place" means the first part of or beginning of something.

Work in pairs. Practice this useful expression from the video.

1 Watch how Alice uses this expression. Then, practice the dialogue below with your partner.

DVD VIDEO CD2 55

Alice: What got you interested in animal rescue **in the first place**?

Elizabeth: I felt like I needed a cause to work for. I love animals and I understand them.

2 Listen to the example dialogue below. Then, practice it with your partner.

DVD AUDIO CD2 56

A: What's your major?

B: My major is <u>economics</u>.

A: I see. What got you interested in that **in the first place**?

B: I got interested in <u>economics</u> because <u>recently the economy has not been so strong in Japan.</u> <u>So, I wanted to study ways to make the economy stronger.</u>

3 Fill in the blanks below with your own ideas. Then, practice the completed dialogue with your partner.

A: What's your major?

B: My major is _____.

A: I see. What got you interested in that **in the first place**?

B: I got interested in _____ because _____

_____

Sharing Your Ideas Doing Volunteer Work

If you did volunteer work, what kind of activity would you like to do? Check (✓) the best activity for you below. Also, write one of your own ideas. Then, compare your ideas with your partner.

If I did volunteer work, I would like to:

☐ care for animals in an animal shelter. ☐ help disabled people.

☐ pick up trash around where I live. ☐ help homeless people.

☐ teach Japanese to foreign students. ☐ volunteer in a home for elderly people.

your idea: _____.

Reading Passage

Can One Person Change the World?

When Elizabeth Oliver was in her thirties, she had a good job teaching at a university. 01
She had a car and a nice home, and enough money to buy whatever she wanted. But 02
even so, she felt that something was missing in her life. She wanted to do something 03
to make the world a better place. This is how she first got involved in animal rescue. In 04
many Western countries, it's common for people to do volunteer work. You may have 05
heard about famous celebrities who support good causes. Hollywood actors Angelina 06
Jolie and Brad Pitt, for example, give their time and money to help children in Africa. 07
But you don't have to be rich or famous to help. In the United States, for example, it's 08
common for average people to do volunteer work, often through school or church 09
groups. Children help too, picking up trash along a river or making sandwiches to 10
distribute to homeless people. As U.S. President Barack Obama once said, "Change 11
will not come if we wait for some other person, or if we wait for some other time." 12
How about you? What cause would you like to support? What can you do in your life 13
today? Do you believe you have the power to change the world?   [212 words] 14

Notes ■ get involved in「…に関わる」 ■ celebrity「有名人」
■ average「平均的な、普通の」 ■ trash「ごみ」 ■ distribute「配る」

- -

Comprehension Check ▷ **Read the sentences below about the passage. Circle True or False.**

1. Elizabeth was happy with her life as a university teacher.   [True / False]
2. Elizabeth first got involved with animal rescue when she was a child.   [True / False]
3. It's common for people in Western countries to do volunteer work.   [True / False]
4. Rich and famous people do more volunteer work than average people.   [True / False]
5. In the United States, even children do volunteer work.   [True / False]

Your Opinions ▷ **Circle the words/phrases in the brackets below to show your opinions. Then, compare your sentences with your partner.**

1. I [have / have never] done volunteer work.
2. In the future, I am [interested / not so interested] in doing volunteer work.
3. If I were rich and famous, I [would / wouldn't] give a lot of my time and money to support good causes.
4. In my opinion, one person [can / cannot] change the world.

Review and Reflect

🎥 Getting Ready

Watch the whole video to get ready for the following activities.

Reviewing the Jobs

Matching Match the pictures on the previous page with the jobs titles below.

[ ] **a.** teacher
[ ] **b.** architect
[ ] **c.** translator
[ ] **d.** tour planner
[ ] **e.** freelance designer
[ ] **f.** marketing director
[ ] **g.** sales representative
[ ] **h.** chief technology officer
[ ] **i.** chef and restaurant owner
[ ] **j.** chair and founder of an NPO
[ ] **k.** president and CEO of a brewery
[ ] **l.** business development manager
[ ] **m.** president of an IT recruiting company
[ ] **n.** assistant supervisor at a convenience store chain

Reflection Discuss your reactions to the different jobs and people in this book with your partner by completing the steps below.

(**Which Job Is Most Interesting?**)

In this book, you watched interviews with 14 professionals with many different kinds of jobs. Which job do you think is the most interesting?

1 Listen to the sample dialogue below. Then, practice it with your partner.

A: We watched interviews with people with many different jobs. Which job seems the most interesting to you?

B: I think being a journalist would be the most interesting job.

A: Really? Of all the different jobs, why did you choose that one?

B: I think that job seems the most interesting because you can meet many interesting people and it's very challenging but exciting.

2 Fill in the blanks with your own ideas. Then, practice the completed dialogue with your partner.

A: We watched interviews with people with many different jobs. Which job seems the most interesting to you?

B: I think being _____ would be the most interesting job.

A: Really? Of all the different jobs, why did you choose that one?

B: I think that job seems the most interesting because _____

_____ and _____

_____.

Who Is a Good Role Model?

In this book, you learned about many successful people who worked hard to get where they are today. Who is a role model for your own career goals?

1 Listen to the sample dialogue below. Then, practice it with your partner.

DVD AUDIO   CD2 60

A: We watched interviews with many successful and inspiring professionals. Who do you think is the best role model for your own career?

B: I think Alice is the best role model for me.

A: Of all the different people, why did you choose her?

B: I think Alice is a good role model because she looks very professional to me. Also, she has been working in Japan for a long time. I would like to work in a foreign country. So, she inspired me.

2 Fill in the blanks with your own ideas. Then, practice the completed dialogue with your partner.

A: We watched interviews with many successful and inspiring professionals. Who do you think is the best role model for your own career?

B: I think _____ is the best role model for me.

A: Of all the different people, why did you choose him/her?

B: I think _____ is a good role model because _____

_____.

Also, _____

_____.

Planning for the Future

Choose one of the questions about your future career and fill in the form below. Then, present your ideas to your classmates. (See the examples on pages 100 and 101.)

1 What sort of work is the best match for you?

2 What one factor do you think is most important when choosing a job?

3 Where do you see yourself in 10 years?

4 What can you do now to prepare for your future career?

5 If you could work in a foreign country, where would you like to work? What job would you like to do there?

. . . .

Your choice: Question number _____

Your answer(s): _____

_____

Reason(s) for your answer(s): _____

_____

_____

Script of Your Presentation

Example Presentations

1   **What sort of work is the best match for you?**

My dream is to be a teacher. I have three reasons why this sort of work is the best match for me. The first reason is I like helping people. Of course being a teacher is one of the best ways to help people. So, this job is perfect for me. The second reason is I care about the future of my country. Teachers have the power to shape future leaders. I want to help in this way. The final reason is my father is also a teacher. So, I think it would be exciting to do the same job as him. We will have many things to talk about.

2   **What one factor do you think is most important when choosing a job?**

For me, the most important factor is finding a job which is challenging. I have many reasons for choosing this factor. First, work is a big part of our lives. We have to spend so much time at the office, so it's important to choose a job which is challenging. If we don't feel challenged, we will get bored easily. Second, some people care only about salary. When I retire, however, I want to think about what I accomplished and not how much money I made. Finally, I was inspired by the people in this book. All of them chose very challenging jobs, but they all seem satisfied with their careers. I want to be like them.

3   **Where do you see yourself in 10 years?**

My dream is to start my own company before I'm 30 years old. I have some good reasons why I would like to start my own company. Many of my friends just want to join a famous company. However, I think Japan is changing. We need more creative people to start their own companies. I would like to be a person like this. I also have some older friends who work for big companies. However, they don't seem satisfied with their jobs. I want to be my own boss. I am an ambitious and creative person, so this is the best future for me. I want to be a leader, not a follower.

4 What can you do now to prepare for your future career?

My goal is to be a great doctor. There are many things I have to do to prepare for this career. One thing I have to do is choose a specialty. The best doctors are specialists, so I have to choose mine. Another thing I have to do is interact with many people. Doctors need to be good at communicating with many kinds of patients, so I need to improve my communication skills. One more thing I have to do is improve my English skills. In the future, it will be more and more important for doctors in Japan to have strong English skills. So, I will continue to study English hard.

5 If you could work in a foreign country, where would you like to work? What job would you like to do there?

I would like to teach Japanese in Australia. There are three main reasons why I chose this job and location. First, I have heard that Japanese is becoming a more popular language in the world to study. So, I think there will be many opportunities to be a Japanese teacher in another country. Second, I would also like to use English. If I live in Australia, I can teach Japanese but also use English every day. It's perfect for me! Third, work-life balance is very important to me. I love scuba diving, so I will have many chances to do this in Australia. When I'm not teaching, I can enjoy my life.

Video Scripts

About This Textbook

Hello, I'm Alice Gordenker, an American journalist living and working in Japan.

For this textbook, I interviewed 14 people from around the world, all of whom live and work in Japan. They represent different professions and different perspectives.

Please watch this video and see what you can learn about working in Japan.

Notes ■ represent「…を代表する」 ■ profession「職業」 ■ perspective「見方、視点」

Unit 1 Sales Can Be Like Acting

Introduction

David White is a sales representative for National Geographic Learning, a publisher of English-learning textbooks. He travels to schools all over Japan, meeting with teachers and recommending materials for their classes.

David is British and grew up in Birmingham. When he was 18, he moved to Liverpool, the hometown of The Beatles.

Until he came to Japan, David was an actor. He traveled all around the world, playing many different roles. The kind of theater he did is called "comedy improvisation." "Improvisation" means performing without a clear advance plan. So each performance is a little different.

David says that experience on stage helps him in his job today. In what way? How could acting be anything like sales?

Notes ■ grow up「成長する」 ■ comedy improvisation「即興喜劇」 ■ advance「事前の」

Interview

T O P I C 1 Play your role well.

Alice: You must spend a lot of time on the road, making sales calls.

David: Yes, spring and fall are my busiest seasons for travel. But at other times of the year, I do spend a lot of time in the office, working with the sales team.

Alice: What kind of work are you doing then?

David: For example, we collect and review sales data. And we look over new products and discuss strategies for promoting them.

Alice: Are you comfortable working in an office where everyone else is Japanese?

David: Absolutely. It's a pleasure to work with Japanese people because they tend to think of others first, not just themselves.

Alice: Everyone always says Japanese are good team players.

David: Yes, I'd say that's true. Each person thinks about what's best for the group. And work is divided so everyone gets opportunities to do what he or she does best.

Alice: So each member of the team has a role to play.

David: Yes, and they play it well.

Notes ■ make a sales call「営業訪問する」 ■ review「精査する、検討する」 ■ look over「…に目を通す」 ■ strategy「戦略」
■ promote「販売促進する」 ■ pleasure「喜び、満足」 ■ tend to *do*「…にする傾向がある」 ■ divide「分ける」

T O P I C 2 ▶ **Think on your feet!**

Alice: Since you make a lot of sales calls, I imagine you're very good at presentations.

David: Presenting information well is definitely an important part of my job, but actually, *listening* is more important.

Alice: Listening is more important? Why is that?

David: If you don't know what the customer needs, you can't provide the right product. You might *think* they want Product A but actually they need Product B.

Alice: So you might waste an entire meeting telling them about something they don't want or need.

David: Indeed. And if you do that, you'll lose the sales opportunity.

Alice: So how do you find out what the customer needs to know?

David: You ask questions and listen carefully to the answers. You can't just memorize the presentation, like a script, and expect to follow it. You have to think on your feet.

Alice: In other words, you have to *improvise*.

David: Exactly! And that's why sales can be a lot like acting.

Notes ■ definitely「確かに、間違いなく」 ■ right「正しい、適切な」 ■ entire「全ての」 ■ script「台本」 ■ follow「従う」
■ think on your feet「すぐに決断する、即答する」 ■ in other words「言い換えれば」

T O P I C 3 ▶ **Be a good listener.**

Alice: In every industry, there's a sales role. Whatever your product is, someone has to sell it. What advice do you have for someone starting out in sales?

David: Be patient. Don't expect to make a sale immediately. It often takes time to seal the deal. Sales is building relationships, which is something we do all our lives. Building long-term relationships takes time. Don't rush things. Patience is a virtue.

Notes ■ make a sale「売れる」 ■ immediately「すぐに」 ■ seal the deal「契約を結ぶ、取引をまとめる」
■ all *one's* life「ずっと」 ■ long-term「長期の」 ■ rush「大急ぎで行う」 ■ virtue「美徳」

Detach from here.

Unit 2 Travel Opens Up the World

Introduction

Merve Ozkok works for H.I.S., one of Japan's leading travel agencies. Right now, she's a tour planner for Central and South America. But actually, Merve is from Turkey!

She has lived in many different cities there. Turkey is a fascinating country where East meets West. In university, Merve studied Japanese and came to Japan four times. For her graduation thesis, she compared the Japanese and Turkish travel industries. By chance, she met the local H.I.S. branch manager. She was so impressed by the company philosophy.

Merve worked for H.I.S. in Istanbul for four years, organizing tours for Japanese people in Turkey. Then in 2014, she transferred to Tokyo headquarters. Now she's preparing to take her career to the next level.

Notes ■ leading「主要な、最大手の」 ■ graduation thesis「卒業論文」 ■ by chance「偶然」
■ philosophy「哲学」 ■ transfer to「…に異動する」 ■ headquarters「本社」

Interview

T O P I C 1 Travel is all about dreams.

Alice: In Istanbul, you organized tours all around Turkey. Is there one place you particularly recommend?

Merve: Cappadocia is very popular. You can ride in a hot air balloon over incredible scenery and stay in a cave hotel.

Alice: Was it your job to make all those arrangements?

Merve: Yes. To make sure all arrangements were in place and that everything went according to plan.

Alice: Problems like a mistake in a hotel reservation or a late bus can spoil a vacation. What did you do to prevent problems from happening?

Merve: I learned to double-check and triple-check everything. I even called the bus drivers in the morning to make sure they were awake.

Alice: You went the extra mile.

Merve: When you're selling travel, you're selling dreams. If just one bus is late, the dream is over.

Alice: Speaking of dreams, what's your goal for the future?

Merve: I'm 27 now. By 30, I want to be a branch manager. The travel industry is tough, but it's so interesting.

Notes ■ incredible scenery「すばらしい景色」 ■ cave「洞窟」 ■ arrangement「手配」 ■ in place「すべて準備万端で」
■ go according to plan「計画通りに進む」 ■ go the extra mile「要求以上の働きをする」 ■ speaking of「…の話と言えば」

Detach from here.

105

T O P I C 2   Big events bring big opportunities.

Alice: So, what kind of work are you doing now?

Merve: I'm planning tours and analyzing countries as possible new destinations.

Alice: What factors do you look at?

Merve: For one thing, I look at infrastructure, to make sure it can support tourism.

Alice: That reminds me—in 2020, Tokyo will host the Olympics. Do you think Japan is ready?

Merve: Not yet. Right now, Japan doesn't have the infrastructure to support so many visitors. We are expecting about 20 million people from overseas.

Alice: That's quite an increase. What needs to be done?

Merve: We need wireless Internet that foreigners can access easily. We also need more signs in English.

Alice: And English speakers, too. All sorts of businesses will need staff who can speak English.

Merve: That's right. And if you join a travel business now, you will be in a great position to do interesting work in 2020.

Alice: It sounds like the Olympics will be a real opportunity for today's young people.

Merve: Absolutely. Big events bring big opportunities.

Notes ■ factor「要素」 ■ remind「…（人）に思い出させる」 ■ host「…を主催する」 ■ sort「種類」

T O P I C 3   Travel makes life more fun.

Alice: People always tell students they should get out and see the world. But really, what can we gain through travel?

Merve: First of all, you see new things and learn new things. Learning new things makes life more fun. You realize that there is more to the world than Japan. And when you travel, you connect with people from different cultures. You see that even when we are different, we are really all the same.

Notes ■ gain「…を得る」 ■ first of all「まず第一に」 ■ realize「…に気が付く、実感する」

Unit 3 Love Sells Cars

Introduction

Tiziana Alamprese is marketing director at Fiat Chrysler Japan. She's responsible for five brands of Italian and American cars. She was born and raised in Italy. What was the family car? A Fiat, of course.

As a teenager, Tiziana became interested in Zen philosophy. She studied Japanese in Naples, at the oldest university in Europe for Asian studies. Later, Tiziana studied economics at Kyushu University. She also earned a *nidan* in kendo.

Tiziana returned to Japan in 2005 to manage Fiat's brands. In 2011, she received an award from the Italian government for her contributions to Italian-Japanese relations. She is a bridge between the two countries.

Notes ■ director「重役」 ■ be responsible for「…に責任がある、…を担当する」 ■ be born and raised「生まれ育つ」
■ economics「経済学」 ■ earn「獲得する」 ■ award「賞」 ■ government「政府」 ■ relation「関係」

Interview

T O P I C 1 A brand is like a baby.

Alice: Your title is "Marketing Director." But really—what is "marketing"?

Tiziana: "Marketing" is what we do to make people love our brand and want to buy our products.

Alice: And your products are cars, right?

Tiziana: Yes. Five brands of cars, including Fiat, Alfa Romeo and Jeep.

Alice: Wow. How do you manage five different brands?

Tiziana: We keep good numbers. For example, my team tracks what drives people to our website. We track test drives. And of course we track orders.

Alice: I see. Numbers are important. What else is necessary?

Tiziana: You see, a brand is like a baby. You have to look at it and see what it needs to grow.

Alice: But you're raising *five* babies—all at the same time!

Tiziana: True. And just as people have their own personalities, each brand has its own needs. So you have to think creatively.

Alice: How do you encourage your team to think outside of the box?

Tiziana: Well, sometimes I sing to them.

Alice: Seriously?

Tiziana: Yes, it helps them find their "inner Italian." Everyone has a little "Italian" in them— their outgoing, crazy side.

Notes ■ including「…を含めて」 ■ personality「個性」 ■ seriously「真剣に、真面目に」
■ inner「隠れた、内面的な」 ■ outgoing「社交的な」

Detach from here.

T O P I C 2 **Sharing creates happiness.**

Alice: You said marketing requires creativity. Can you give me an example?

Tiziana: The Fiat Caffé. It was the first car café in Japan.

Alice: And it was your idea?

Tiziana: Yes, when I started this job, awareness of our brand was very low in Japan. Sales to women were especially low. The problem was that women don't go to showrooms.

Alice: Ah, but they do go to cafés!

Tiziana: Exactly. So they go to the café, they have a good time, they see our car, and they see our brand.

Alice: Is your strategy working?

Tiziana: Now women buy more than half of our cars. Each month the café has a new theme. We collaborate with other Italian brands. And we love to share the space with the NPOs that we support.

Alice: "Share with Fiat." That's one of your marketing phrases.

Tiziana: Yes, because we need to think about everyone's happiness, not just our own. It's through sharing that we create true happiness for everyone.

Notes   ■ require「…を必要とする」 ■ theme「テーマ」 ■ collaborate with「…と協力する、連携する」

T O P I C 3 **Give yourself a smile.**

Alice: You have a really tough job but you always seem so positive. What's your secret?

Tiziana: Ah, it's my "Smile Project." Every morning, I take a picture of myself with a big smile on my face.

Alice: Really? Why?

Tiziana: Because you have to take care of yourself. You have to love yourself. Of course I have troubles. But I don't let them crush me. If you respect yourself, you will be respected by others. So give yourself a smile, every day.

Notes   ■ take care of「…を保護する、大切にする」 ■ respect「…を気遣う」

Detach from here.

Translating Is More Than Words

Introduction

Alexander O. Smith is an American who lives in Kamakura. He is married and has two children.

Alex works as a translator of books and games. He started his career at Square Enix, then set up his own translation agency. He also founded a publishing company so more people can read Japanese books in English. Right now, he's working on a detective story by Higashino Keigo.

When Alex was a child, he loved fantasy role-playing games like Dungeons & Dragons. He even wrote his own games. Alex became interested in foreign languages because his parents ran a hotel. Guests came from all over the world. In high school, he was an exchange student in China. Later he learned Japanese, too.

All these experiences helped Alex later in life.

Notes ■ translator「翻訳家」 ■ found「…を設立する」 ■ a publishing company「出版社」
■ an exchange student「交換留学生」 ■ experience「経験」

Interview

 Learn your strengths.

Alice: Alex, you've done a lot of translations.

Alex: I have. More than 40 games and books.

Alice: This one looks like it must have been pretty difficult. How did you learn Japanese so well?

Alex: I studied words in context. Words have a wide range of meaning. You can't learn that from a dictionary. That's why context is so important.

Alice: You mean, how the words are used?

Alex: That's right. For example, I watched television. When I came across a word I didn't know, I wrote it down, along with the full sentence or situation.

Alice: Would that work for learning English, too?

Alex: It works for any language.

Alice: You must have been a good student.

Alex: Well, in college I always took as many classes as I could. And I met a lot of people. If I had even a slight interest in something, I explored it.

Alice: So, you had a wide range of experiences.

Alex: College is a great place to explore different interests. That's how you learn your strengths.

Notes ■ pretty「かなり」 ■ a wide range of「幅広い…」 ■ work「うまくいく」 ■ slight「わずかな」

Detach from here.

T O P I C 2 **You have to translate the experience.**

Alice: I've never met anyone who translates games before. It must be interesting.

Alex: It is. But with games we don't call it "translating." We call it "localizing."

Alice: "Localizing"? What does that mean?

Alex: It means recreating the game in another culture. It's more than just translating words.

Alice: I'm not sure I understand. Can you give me an example?

Alex: Sure. I localized a game called Final Fantasy X. In one important scene, a boy and a girl are at the end of a long journey. They've been through a lot together. In the Japanese version, she turns to him and says, "Arigato."

Alice: So, "Thank you."?

Alex: I couldn't use "thank you" here. The scene would have lost its power. In this context, "thank you" isn't the same as "arigato."

Alice: How *did* you translate it?

Alex: "I love you."

Alice: Ah, because feelings are expressed more directly in English.

Alex: Right. Translating is more than words. You have to translate the experience.

Notes ■ localize「…を特定の国や地域に適用できるように改変する」 ■ journey「(長い)旅」 ■ directly「直接的に」

T O P I C 3 **Sometimes plans change.**

Alice: You went to graduate school planning to become a professor. But after two years, you changed your plan. Wasn't that a little bit scary?

Alex: No, because I knew my strengths. I was good at computers. I was good at languages. And I understood games.

Alice: You found a career that uses your strengths.

Alex: Everybody is good at something. If you explore your interests, you'll find your strengths.

Notes ■ scary「怖い」

Unit **5** Serve Up the Best Possible Service

Introduction

Lam Thanh Huyen works at Lawson, one of Japan's largest convenience store chains. She is an assistant supervisor in a group in charge of 140 stores in central Tokyo.

Lam is Vietnamese. Her father is an international businessman, and her older sister works in Vietnam's foreign ministry. Watching them, Lam became interested in English and other foreign languages.

Initially, she wanted to go to university in the United States or England. She heard about Ritsumeikan Asia Pacific University in Oita. Lam applied there because she could study not only English but also Japanese, and learn about Japan.

She convinced her parents to let her go by promising to return to Vietnam one day. Lam is gaining valuable knowledge and experience at Lawson. When she goes home, what does she want to take back to her country?

Notes ■ foreign ministry「外務省」 ■ apply「志願する」 ■ valuable「貴重な」 ■ knowledge「知識」

Interview

T O P I C **1** Process information quickly.

Alice: When you first joined the company, you worked in Natural Lawson stores. Now you're in store management. What's your typical week like?

Lam: On Monday, we meet to discuss new products. Every week, we introduce about 100 new products.

Alice: How do you manage so many at once?

Lam: New items go into stores on Tuesday. On Wednesday, we call the stores with first-day sales data to help them plan their orders.

Alice: You're processing information very quickly.

Lam: We have to. Convenience stores work on very small margins. We need to use every centimeter for products that sell.

Alice: How about the rest of your week?

Lam: On Thursday and Friday, I visit the stores to see how they are doing, and give them advice.

Alice: You're so young. You're working in a foreign language. How do you convince store managers to listen to you?

Lam: That's the most difficult part of my job. I'm always trying to learn better ways to say things, so I can be more convincing.

Notes ■ store management「店舗管理」 ■ typical「典型的な、標準的な」
■ process「…を処理する」 ■ margin「利益」 ■ convincing「説得力のある」

T O P I C 2 Show customers that you care.

Alice: I've noticed that convenience stores are selling fresh-made coffee now.

Lam: When I visit one of our stores, the first thing I do is check the "MACHI café" corner.

Alice: Coffee is that important?

Lam: It's the most profitable item. Just for "MACHI café," I have a check list with 17 items.

Alice: That's a careful check.

Lam: Of course I check the taste. But I also watch how the staff interacts with customers.

Alice: Even in a convenience store, you're providing individual customer service.

Lam: Yes, because it's an opportunity to have a conversation with our customers, and show them "omoiyari."

Alice: Consideration. To show that you care.

Lam: When we hand customers their coffee, we say, "熱いですから、お気をつけください." "It's hot, so please take care." Then, we give them a nice smile.

Alice: Terrific customer service. That's one reason I love Japan.

Lam: It's so warm and friendly. I want people in my country to experience Japanese customer service.

Notes ■ notice「…に気が付く」 ■ care「気遣う」 ■ take care「気を付ける、注意する」

T O P I C 3 It's OK to ask for help.

Alice: When you were looking for a job, did you know you wanted to work in the service industry?

Lam: No. At first, I just looked at companies doing business in Vietnam. I interviewed with manufacturers and trading companies, but I didn't get any offers. I asked my teacher for advice. She helped me realize that I love connecting with people. I've got the right personality for customer service. If you're feeling stuck, it's OK to ask for help. It worked for me.

Notes ■ interview with「…の面接を受ける」 ■ manufacturer「(大規模な)製造業者、メーカー」
■ trading company「商社」 ■ right「適した」 ■ ask for「…を求める」

Toast Your Success!

Introduction

Shigeharu Asagiri is the president of Coedo Brewery in Kawagoe, Saitama Prefecture. His company makes prize-winning beers including one made from a famous local product—sweet potatoes.

Shigeharu had a typical Japanese upbringing, attending local schools. He has never lived or studied outside Japan.

Shigeharu wanted to start his own business one day, so at Hitotsubashi University, he studied accounting and business development. He traveled twice a year during school vacations, backpacking all over Europe and Asia. In Germany, Shigeharu was amazed by the huge variety of beers.

Today, he calls himself a "beer evangelist," shipping his unique beers to countries throughout the world. But how did such a local product go global?

Notes ■ upbringing「教育（法）」 ■ accounting「会計学」 ■ business development「事業開発」 ■ huge variety of「膨大な種類の…」 ■ amazed「驚いた」 ■ evangelist「伝道師」 ■ ship「輸送する」 ■ throughout the world「世界中で」

Interview

TOPIC 1 **Hard work pays off.**

Alice: Beniaka is the world's first beer made from sweet potatoes. Where did you get the idea?

Shigeharu: Our company started as a distributor of organic vegetables.

Alice: Including Kawagoe's famous sweet potatoes?

Shigeharu: Yeah, we were looking for a way to use the ones that are too small to be sold.

Alice: Giving value to a product that would normally be thrown out.

Shigeharu: It took a lot of trial and error, but we finally developed a recipe that worked.

Alice: And just in time for the "ji-biru boom," when local beers were popular.

Shigeharu: Yes, but the boom didn't last because the quality of "ji-biru" was inconsistent. Consumers went back to mass-produced beer, and we had to restructure our business.

Alice: What specific steps did you take?

Shigeharu: We cut our product line from over 100 beers to just five.

Alice: And you redesigned your labels and marketing message, right?

Shigeharu: We repositioned our brand from a "ji-biru" to a craft beer, emphasizing quality.

Alice: Your hard work seems to have paid off. We should toast your success.

Shigeharu: Thank you. Now we are one of the biggest small breweries in Japan.

Notes ■ distributor「卸売業者」 ■ just in time for「…にちょうど間に合うように」 ■ last「持続する」 ■ inconsistent「一貫性のない」 ■ restructure「…を再構築する」 ■ reposition「…を別の位置へ移す」 ■ emphasize「…を強調する」

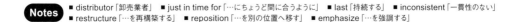

T O P I C 2 **COEDO beer goes overseas.**

Alice: Your company is a small producer. Wouldn't it be better to focus on the domestic market? Why go overseas?

Shigeharu: I'll go anywhere I have customers. Our beer is enjoyed in many countries, including the United States, South Korea and France.

Alice: So you see the whole world as your market?

Shigeharu: Of course. Exports are about 15 percent of our business.

Alice: And you've won all these awards. Why do you think your beer does so well in international competitions?

Shigeharu: Do you know the Japanese word *monozukuri*?

Alice: "Craftsmanship"?

Shigeharu: Yes, but it also means "attention to detail" and "continuous improvement."

Alice: A commitment to do your best.

Shigeharu: That's right. People in other countries appreciate that COEDO is hand-crafted, high-quality, *Japanese* beer.

Alice: I'm sure the awards helped your domestic business, too.

Shigeharu: Definitely. Winning international awards raised our profile in Japan dramatically.

Notes ■ competition「コンペ、品評会」　■ craftsmanship「職人技」　■ attention「配慮」　■ continuous「継続的な」
■ appreciate「認識する」　■ hand-crafted「手づくりの」　■ profile「(会社の)評判、イメージ」　■ dramatically「劇的に」

T O P I C 3 **Just try again.**

Alice: You've only studied English in Japan. And you describe your English as *konjo eigo* (根性英語). What does that mean?

Shigeharu: It means I don't give up.

Alice: You keep trying.

Shigeharu: Because I have to. Because I have something I need to communicate.

Alice: What strategies do you use when someone doesn't understand your English?

Shigeharu: I try using a different word. Or I write down what I want to say. Sometimes I use the Internet. If someone doesn't understand you the first time, don't feel embarrassed. Just try again.

Notes ■ describe「…を言い表す」

Detach from here.

Unit 7   Teaching Is Helping Others Perform Their Best

Introduction

Andrew Wakatsuki-Robinson is from New Zealand. He teaches English at Shukutoku Elementary School in Tokyo.

He grew up in a big family, one of five children. His parents were very laid-back. They encouraged their children to follow their dreams, but they never pushed. In university, Andrew majored in theater and music. These are still his passions, and he often uses them in his teaching.

When Andrew is not at school, he's directing theater. He puts on plays with English-speaking actors from many different countries. Right now, he's adapting Yamagata folk tales for the stage, so they can be performed in English for audiences in London.

Whether teaching or directing, Andrew takes the laid-back approach he learned from his parents. How does that play out in the classroom?

Notes ■ major in「…を専攻する」 ■ theater「演劇」 ■ passion「熱中するもの」
■ put on「…を上演する」 ■ folk tale「民話」 ■ audience「観客」

Interview

T O P I C 1   Children learn in different ways.

Alice: Children are a tough audience. How do you keep your students' attention in the classroom?

Andrew: Children learn in different ways. Some children absorb information better if they see it. Some children learn best by writing, and others need to move around.

Alice: How do you cope with so many different learning styles?

Andrew: I try a variety of teaching tools, and see what works best for the class. And I change activities frequently.

Alice: You said, "teaching tools." Can you give me an example?

Andrew: I can give you three. One very important tool is music. If children like a song, they will want to learn the words so they can sing along.

Alice: Songs are also a good way to learn the natural rhythm of English.

Andrew: That's true. Another good tool is technology. When children are interacting, they are learning.

Alice: That's two. What's the third?

Andrew: Competition. For some children, competition is a powerful motivator. When they see another child doing something well, they want to do it well, too.

Notes ■ a variety of「様々な…」 ■ frequently「頻繁に」 ■ tool「手段」 ■ along「一緒に」

T O P I C ❷ Give people options to try out.

Alice: At school, you teach children. On stage, you direct adults. Is that very different?

Andrew: Teaching and directing are both about helping others perform their best.

Alice: How do you do that? How do you bring out the best in other people's performances?

Andrew: First, I look for something I can praise. I say something like, "I like the way you did that."

Alice: That must make them feel good.

Andrew: It does. And it gets their attention. Once I've got them listening, I can ask questions, like, "How can you sharpen that up?"

Alice: I see. You challenge them to think for themselves.

Andrew: When directing, I often have ideas about how to improve a scene. But rather than telling the actors how I think we should improve the scene, I suggest we try the scene three ways.

Alice: Including the way you think it should be done?

Andrew: You picked that, did you? Well, they are more likely to accept an idea if they've tested it themselves. Sometimes another way proves best, and that's fine. Then, we go with that. I do the same thing in the classroom.

Notes ■ sharpen ... up「…をより良くする」 ■ challenge ... to *do*「…（人）が～するよう意欲をかきたてる」
■ pick「…を見つける、…に気付く」 ■ go with「…を選ぶ」

T O P I C ❸ Don't tell; ask!

Alice: In any job, there are opportunities to teach, whether it's explaining a product to a client or orienting new employees. Can you share some hints about how to teach well?

Andrew: First of all, nobody likes to be told they're doing something wrong. Don't criticize; instead, make a positive comment. Next, ask questions, like, "What else could you do?" When you help people see their work more clearly, they will find ways to improve it. Teaching is helping others perform their best.

Notes ■ orient「…を適応させる」 ■ instead「代わりに」

Unit 8 Build a Happy Life!

Introduction

Astrid Klein is an architect who has been working in Japan for 25 years. She's also trained in interior design.

Astrid is German but was born in Italy. As a child, she went to a truly international school. She studied history in French, math in German and art in Italian!

Astrid went to university in France, and graduate school in England. While training to become an architect, she met her business partner, Mark Dytham. Astrid and Mark came to Japan together in 1988. Two years later, they set up Klein Dytham architecture.

They design buildings that are both impressive and playful. Each building is so different. What do they have in common? They're all fun!

Notes ■ truly「本当に、真に」 ■ impressive「印象的な」

Interview

T O P I C 1 Be open to new things.

Alice: You speak five languages. You could work anywhere in the world. Why did you choose Japan?

Astrid: Japan seemed very exciting. In university, we would look through architectural magazines...and the buildings in Japan were all so wild and crazy!

Alice: You thought you could do interesting work in Japan?

Astrid: Europe is more conservative. We have beautiful old cities, but no one wants to change anything. It's very hard to design new buildings.

Alice: So, after graduate school, you came to Japan. How was it?

Astrid: Two things impressed me. One was the quality of work. And the other was the use of innovative materials.

Alice: Why are those important?

Astrid: Because in Japan you can make things that would be difficult to make in other countries.

Alice: So you see Japan as a land of possibility?

Astrid: Absolutely. Japanese people are very open to new things.

Notes ■ wild「独特の、面白い」 ■ impress「感心させる」 ■ material「材料」

T O P I C ❷ Challenge is fun.

Alice: In your work, what's important to you?

Astrid: I want to do new things. And I want to have fun.

Alice: So which of your recent projects was both new and fun?

Astrid: The Tsutaya bookstore.

Alice: In Daikanyama?

Astrid: Yes. Tsutaya is famous for its T mark. So we used that in our design. There are three big Ts on the outside of the building. And smaller Ts on the walls.

Alice: That is fun. What was new?

Astrid: On this project, we were asked to design the interior as well. And even how the products are displayed.

Alice: That's more than architects usually do. Wasn't it difficult?

Astrid: Sure, but things that come easily aren't fun. You have to struggle. You have to sweat. It's the challenging work that's fun.

Notes ■ as well「おまけに、…も」 ■ struggle「奮闘する、苦労する」 ■ sweat「汗をかく」

T O P I C ❸ Be honest with yourself.

Alice: You really enjoy your work. How can someone find work they enjoy?

Astrid: Only you know what makes you happy. So you have to be honest with yourself. If you like doing something, you'll do it well. You'll be passionate about it. Don't hide your passion. Let people see it. And put your modesty away. If you want a happy life, you have to build it yourself. No one will build it for you.

Notes ■ hide「隠す」 ■ put ... away「…を捨てる」 ■ modesty「慎み深さ、謙遜」

Detach from here

Unit 9 Life Is Like Riding a Bicycle

Introduction

Sachiko Takao is a freelance website designer and online advertising consultant. She lives and works in a "social apartment," where residents have their own rooms but come together in shared living and work spaces.

Sachi is from Fukuoka. She's the only daughter in her family, but her mother, who spent two years abroad, encouraged Sachi to see the world. Sachi spent a year of high school in California, and found it so exciting that she went back to the U.S. for university. She majored in cinema and television arts. She earned college credit doing internships at major broadcasters, including NHK Los Angeles.

Sachi built a successful career in the U.S. and the U.K. But she felt like something was missing. She decided to make a bike trip from Okinawa to Hokkaido to find local foods and introduce them to the world.

On that trip, she discovered what she wants to do next *and* what she can contribute to Japan. What is it?

Notes ■ resident「住民」 ■ bike「自転車」 ■ discover「…を発見する、…が分かる」 ■ contribute to「…に貢献する」

Interview

 Freelancing is flexible.

Alice: When you worked overseas, you were employed by major companies, including Disney. Here in Japan, you're self-employed.

Sachi: Yup, I'm freelancing.

Alice: What kind of projects are you working on now?

Sachi: My main client is a manufacturer of bicycle frames designed especially for triathlons.

Alice: That's a very specialized product.

Sachi: Right, so we have to do very targeted marketing. I created a global brand image for them, starting from zero, including a website and social media, like Facebook and Twitter.

Alice: How many people does it take to manage all that?

Sachi: Me, myself and I.

Alice: Ah, you do everything yourself!

Sachi: Yes. And on top of that, I go to events, like the IRONMAN World Championship in Hawaii, where I meet the athletes directly.

Alice: That sounds like a lot of fun. Is that why you decided to work freelance?

Sachi: Hey, freelancing is not all fun and games. No, actually, working freelance gives me time to work on my own projects, too. I can focus on what's coming next.

Notes ■ self-employed「自営業の」 ■ specialized「専門の」 ■ Me, myself and I「自分だけ」(自分を強調する口語表現)

Detach from here.

T O P I C 2   Being with people is important.

Alice: You spent seven months cycling the whole length of Japan. And it was on that trip that you decided what you want to do next?

Sachi: That's right. I was keeping a blog about my journey. I thought I was writing for people overseas, but it turned out Japanese people were reading my blog too, to learn English.

Alice: And you realized you could turn blogging into a business?

Sachi: I realized Japan needs fun and interesting ways to learn English. Japan needs people like me, who love life and love English.

Alice: So what's your plan?

Sachi: I'm still working on that, but I'm thinking about a podcast. Maybe with sponsors, and different contributors. We can cover all kinds of topics, from music to business.

Alice: You've got a lot of interesting ideas.

Sachi: I talk about it a lot! I get great ideas from the people I live with.

Alice: Living in a "social apartment" is perfect for you. This is a great place to incubate your plan.

Sachi: Being with people is important. When you're with other people, you feed each other ideas.

 Notes ■ cycle「自転車で旅行する」 ■ length「長さ」 ■ keep a blog「ブログを書く」 ■ turn out「…であることが分かる」
■ contributor「寄付者、協賛者」 ■ incubate「…を生み出す、練る」 ■ feed「…を与える、提供する」

T O P I C 3   Keep moving!

Alice: You've done a lot of adventurous things—living abroad, taking a bike trip alone, and now you're planning to start a business. Don't you ever get afraid?

Sachi: Of course I do. I have fears, like everyone else. It's scary when I don't know where I'm going or what I should do. But "Life is like riding a bicycle. To keep your balance, you have to keep moving." Einstein said that. And it's so true. If you keep moving, you will get past your fears.

Unit 10 Trade Ideas for Positive Change

Introduction

Christopher Faulkner works for Mitsui & Co., Ltd., a major Japanese trading company. He's working on innovative energy projects.

He was born and raised in Australia, where he started studying Japanese when he was 12 years old. When he was young, he dreamed of using science to make the world a better place. After high school, he took a "gap year" and backpacked all around Europe. When he returned to Australia, he went to university and earned a double degree in Japanese and engineering.

Later, Chris did his master's degree at Tokyo University. He studied polymers that can capture gasses. Chris considered a career in pure research, but decided he'd rather work with other people.

Chris joined Mitsui & Co., Ltd. in 2011. Is he living his dream? Is he using science to make the world a better place?

Notes ■ degree「学位」 ■ master's degree「修士号」 ■ polymer「ポリマー、高分子化合物」
■ consider「検討する」 ■ live「…を実践する」

Interview

T O P I C 1 A big company offers big possibilities.

Alice: Mitsui is a really giant company, with thousands of employees and offices in more than 60 countries.

Chris: That was attractive to me. A big company offers big possibilities.

Alice: What sort of possibilities?

Chris: I saw a lot of room for growth for me personally, but also room for me to actively participate and contribute to the company.

Alice: How important was it to you that Mitsui is a multinational company?

Chris: Very important. I knew I wanted to work globally. And since joining Mitsui, I *have* worked in many different countries, including China, the United States and Germany.

Alice: So Mitsui brings together all sorts of people and technology.

Chris: When you combine talent and resources from all over the world, you can do things that have never been done before. The impossible becomes possible.

Notes ■ attractive「心を引き付ける、魅力的な」 ■ room「余地、機会、可能性」 ■ participate「参加する」
■ talent「才能」 ■ the impossible「不可能なこと」(〈the ＋形容詞〉で名詞化)

T O P I C 2 Put your knowledge to work.

Alice: At Tokyo University, you did interesting research about gasses. Are you using that knowledge now in your job?

Chris: Absolutely. One of the projects I'm working on now involves a new technology that can capture carbon dioxide from waste gas and turn it into a liquid fuel.

Alice: That sounds like a double benefit.

Chris: Exactly. It's good for the environment because it reduces CO_2 emissions. At the same time, it creates a new source of energy that's both cheap and clean.

Alice: And energy in liquid form is relatively easy to transport and trade.

Chris: That's right. This technology would be particularly useful in countries like China, Russia and India. All these countries need affordable ways to reduce CO_2 emissions. They also need clean sources of energy.

Alice: These are urgent needs, aren't they?

Chris: Yes, they are. And I expect today's students will come up with other innovative solutions.

Notes ■ involve「…を伴う」 ■ carbon dioxide「二酸化炭素」 ■ waste gas「排ガス」 ■ liquid「液体」 ■ environment「環境」
■ emission「排出」 ■ relatively「比較的」 ■ transport「輸送する」 ■ affordable「値段が手頃な」 ■ solution「解決策」

T O P I C 3 Change the world with the power of many.

Alice: When students are thinking about their future careers, everyone tells them to follow their passion. But you found your path by thinking about what you *didn't* want to do.

Chris: That's right. I knew I didn't want to work alone. I knew I wanted to work with people. So I looked for a job where I could join forces with others. Aristotle said, "The whole is greater than the sum of its parts." When you work with others, you can accomplish more than you can accomplish alone. With the power of many, it *is* possible to change the world.

Notes ■ path「道筋、方向、方針」 ■ force「(共同作業のための)集団」 ■ sum「合計」

Detach from here.

Unit 11 Connect Workers With Companies

Introduction

Annie Chang is the president of an IT recruiting company. She helps companies find workers with computer skills.

She was born and raised in Taiwan. Her first job was teaching in a high school. In 1981, Annie came to Japan, looking for adventure. She didn't have a job. She didn't speak Japanese. She had to make her own opportunities. When she worked in a computer store, she learned English so she could help customers from other countries.

Annie saw a need for IT services in English, so in 1989, she started her own company. At that time, IT recruiting was still unusual in Japan. Annie was a pioneer and her success attracted the attention of magazines and newspapers from all over the world.

Leaving her own country helped Annie discover her strengths. Now she helps others by connecting good workers with good companies.

Notes　■ unusual「珍しい」　■ attract「引き付ける」　■ attention「注目」　■ leave「…を去る、離れる」

Interview

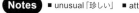 **Get out of your comfort zone.**

Alice: You have both foreign and Japanese clients.
Annie: Yes. Most of my clients are in technology, health care and financial services.
Alice: What are these companies looking for?
Annie: Technical skills. Today, all companies need people who can develop and support business applications.
Alice: Where do you find workers with good technical skills?
Annie: I recruit from all over the world. Programmers are coming to Japan from so many different countries, including the United States, India and Vietnam. They are all ambitious and want to succeed.
Alice: So Japan's employment market is already global. Can young Japanese compete?
Annie: Honestly? Many of them cannot. Young Japanese are too comfortable these days. Everything is just handed to them.
Alice: So, what's the solution?
Annie: They need to challenge themselves more and get out of their comfort zone, or they will never go anywhere.

Notes　■ employment「雇用」　■ hand「…を渡す」

T O P I C 2 **If you try, people will help you.**

Alice: You've helped thousands of people find jobs. In interviews, what are companies really looking for in a candidate?

Annie: The number one thing is attitude.

Alice: Attitude?

Annie: Yes, all companies want people with a positive attitude. People who are motivated and passionate.

Alice: What else is important?

Annie: Communication skills. These days, companies are operating all over the globe. Your software is written in India. Your manufacturing is in China. Your testing is in Malaysia. Companies need staff who can communicate with people from all over the world.

Alice: In English, right?

Annie: Yes, but the desire to communicate is more important than how well you speak. If people see you trying to communicate, they will help you by trying to understand. What it really comes down to is attitude.

Notes ■ interview「面接」 ■ motivated「やる気のある」 ■ operate「事業を行う」
■ manufacturing「製造」 ■ come down to「…に帰着する、最終的に…に落ち着く」

T O P I C 3 **Try this method for relaxed interviews.**

Alice: Many students get really nervous in interviews. How can they get past that?

Annie: I have a great method. First, make eye contact. That makes you look confident and feel confident. Next, smile. A smile relaxes you. And it relaxes the other person, too.

Alice: Hmmm. Smiling and making eye contact. Those aren't always easy for Japanese people.

Annie: They can get used to it. I tell my recruits to practice...with a mirror.

Notes ■ get used to「…に慣れる」 ■ recruit「求職者」

Detach from here.

Unit 12 Necessity Is the Mother of Invention

Introduction

This man's name is Sreekumar Bhanuvikraman Pillai Ambika. He is chief technology officer at EP Consulting Services in Tokyo. Sreekumar manages an international team of engineers and programmers who develop IT solutions for other companies.

Sreekumar came to Japan in 2002 from India. He studied engineering at one of the best universities in his country. Ever since high school, Sreekumar had his sights set on a career in information technology. He taught himself computer languages like Cobol and Basic. But his family couldn't afford a computer. So he asked a local business owner to buy him one. In exchange, he promised to write programs to improve the man's business.

That's initiative! How does this enterprising engineer use IT in his job and life today?

Notes ■ have *one's* sights set on「…を狙っている」 ■ cannot afford「…を買う余裕がない」
■ in exchange「引き換えに」 ■ initiative「進取の精神、独創力、自発性、率先」

Interview

T O P I C 1 **There's always room to innovate.**

Alice: You're a manager now. Does that mean you're not programming anymore?

Sreekumar: No, I still program, too. In fact, I played a big role in developing the system I used to reserve this room today.

Alice: How does it work?

Sreekumar: There is a tablet computer outside each room where you can check in, check out or make a reservation for later. We also have a central screen where you can see the status of all the rooms at once.

Alice: Oh, that's very convenient.

Sreekumar: We developed the system for internal use for our company only, but clients from other companies saw it and wanted it for their offices, too.

Alice: So, you turned it into a product.

Sreekumar: That's right. Eventually, we sold it to another company that is placing it in offices all over the country. We're adding new features, like the ability to pre-set lighting or audio sound.

Alice: You saw a need, and you developed a solution.

Sreekumar: "Necessity is the mother of invention." There's always room to innovate.

Notes ■ status「状況」 ■ at once「一度に」 ■ internal「内部の」 ■ eventually「結局、最終的に」
■ place「…を設置する」 ■ feature「機能」 ■ pre-set「…を予め設定する」 ■ innovate「革新する」

TOPIC 2 Technology brings people together.

Alice: You first came to Japan in 2002. Did you have trouble adjusting to life in a new country?

Sreekumar: At first I was a little homesick. The weather was cold and I wasn't used to the food. Also, I didn't speak any Japanese.

Alice: Did you seek out other Indians for support?

Sreekumar: I tried, but it wasn't so easy then. There wasn't even a website for the Indian community. So I created one.

Alice: A perfect use for your skills.

Sreekumar: The website was a catalyst for the community to become more active. Now we organize many festivals and events where we share Indian culture.

Alice: You even have Indian movie nights. Can anyone come?

Sreekumar: Oh, yes. Everyone is welcome. Indian movies have wonderful singing and dancing.

Alice: I love the way you use technology not just in your job, but for the community, too.

Sreekumar: Technology has the power to bring people together. And it can make things happen.

Notes ■ catalyst「触媒、きっかけ、刺激」 ■ way「やり方、考え方」

TOPIC 3 Take initiative.

Alice: Students today use a lot of IT in their daily lives, from smart cards to smart phones.

Sreekumar: Yes, but it's a waste to use technology just for games and entertainment. Those are powerful devices. Instead, ask yourself, "How does the train company know if I have money on my card?" Then, think about how you can use technology in *your* life. Don't be passive; take initiative.

Notes ■ entertainment「娯楽」

Detach from here.

Unit 13 What's the Recipe for Success?

Introduction

Philippe Batton is a French chef who owns two popular restaurants in Tokyo. Le Petit Tonneau—casual bistros offering French food at affordable prices.

Philippe started training as a chef when he was just 16 years old. Within a few years, he worked his way up to the kitchen of one of the best hotels in Paris. In 1986, Philippe spent a year in Kobe. Four years later, he returned to Japan, and decided to make it his home. In 1996, he challenged a famous chef on the TV show, "Ryori no Tetsujin"—and won!

He appears at practically every event in Japan to promote French food and wine. He's published cookbooks in Japanese with easy recipes that anyone can make at home. The French government has honored him for his efforts.

Now Philippe is a leader in the industry. What's his recipe for success?

Notes
- practically 「ほとんど」(直後の語を修飾して、「(…も)同然」のニュアンス)
- honor「…に栄誉を与える」 ■ effort「努力(すること)」 ■ recipe「コツ、秘訣」

Interview

 Go for it!

Alice: You came to Japan for the first time when you were still in your twenties. How did you get that first opportunity?

Philippe: I was in the right place at the right time. I was working at a restaurant in Paris, and my boss needed someone to train Japanese chefs in Kobe.

Alice: What were your first impressions of Japan?

Philippe: I thought the level of cooking was very high. People in Japan respect the ingredients, and they respect their tools. I liked that.

Alice: Was there anything you *didn't* like?

Philippe: I didn't like that French food was so expensive. It was out of reach for most people.

Alice: So you made it your goal to introduce *casual* French food?

Philippe: In France, we have casual restaurants called "bistro." But there was nothing like that in Japan then. I saw a niche in the market.

Alice: Wasn't it risky to try something that had never been done before?

Philippe: There are always risks when you do something new. But when I see an opportunity, I go for it.

Notes
- niche「(成功する可能性のある市場の)隙間、特定分野、ニッチ」
- go for「…を得ようと努める、目指す」(go for itには成句として「頑張ってやってみる」という意味もある)

Detach from here.

T O P I C 2 **If you don't give, you don't get.**

Alice: You volunteer a lot of your time going to events to promote French food and wine. Wouldn't it be better to focus on your own restaurants?

Philippe: I do focus. I cook and I am in my restaurants every day. But every event is an opportunity to share French culture.

Alice: And that's your mission? To share French culture with Japan?

Philippe: Yes. And food is a window on culture. Whenever I can, I want to open that window and show people real French cuisine.

Alice: How, specifically, do you do that?

Philippe: For one thing, I teach at cooking schools all over Japan. And I collaborate with various companies to create special events.

Alice: You really seem to enjoy being with people.

Philippe: I do. I love people. And when you're out and meeting people, you get new opportunities.

Alice: So helping others is one part of your recipe for success.

Philippe: If you don't give, you don't get.

Notes ■ volunteer「…を進んで与える」 ■ mission「(自らに課した)使命」 ■ specifically「具体的には」 ■ various「様々な」

T O P I C 3 **Life is like a chessboard.**

Alice: You're a well-known chef. Your restaurants are successful. Things seem really good for you right now.

Philippe: Yes, but it hasn't all been easy. I've had to work hard. I'm always at work when everyone else is off—evenings, weekends and holidays. And sometimes I fail. But life is like a chessboard. Sometimes you land on a black square. But even then, there are white squares all around you. There's always a way to move forward.

Notes ■ chessboard「チェス盤」 ■ land on「…に降りる」 ■ square「(チェス盤の)目、ます」 ■ forward「前方へ」

Unit 14 Help Animals for a Better Society

Introduction

Elizabeth Oliver is founder and chair of ARK—Animal Refuge Kansai. This NPO cares for homeless pets while trying to find them new homes.

Elizabeth is originally from England, where she grew up with dogs, cats, and even a pony of her own. Her mother taught her responsibility towards animals. Elizabeth was not allowed to eat dinner until all the pets were fed.

Elizabeth came to Japan "out of curiosity" when she was 25 years old. She has lived in Kansai for nearly half a century. Since founding ARK in 1990, she and her supporters have rescued thousands of cats and dogs. In 2012, she was awarded Britain's highest honor for charitable work.

Elizabeth has big plans for the future, including this brand new shelter in Sasayama, Hyogo. It is the most modern shelter in Japan, and a showcase for world-class standards in animal welfare.

Notes ■ founder「創設者」 ■ chair「理事長」 ■ refuge「避難所」 ■ allow ... to do「…(人)に〜することを許す」
■ feed「…にえさを与える」(fed は過去形) ■ out of curiosity「好奇心から」 ■ showcase「試験的に披露する場」

Interview

T O P I C 1 Find a cause to work for.

Alice: It's been almost 25 years since you founded ARK. In that time, how many animals have you rescued?

Elizabeth: More than 4,000 dogs and close to 2,000 cats. We needed more capacity, which is why we built this new facility.

Alice: What got you interested in animal rescue in the first place?

Elizabeth: I felt like I needed a cause to work for. I love animals and I understand them. In Japan, I saw a lot of injured animals but no system to help them.

Alice: In Western countries, there are shelters that will take in pets when their owners can't keep them.

Elizabeth: That's right. I wanted to bring that kind of safety net to Japan, and show that it's possible to find new homes for pets.

Alice: That's a nice way to give back to Japan.

Elizabeth: There are so many good causes to work for. We all have the capacity to contribute to society.

Notes ■ close to「ほぼ…」 ■ capacity「収容力、能力・資質」(後者は2つ目の capacity の意味) ■ facility「施設」

Detach from here.

T O P I C 2 **There's always a solution.**

Alice: The Kobe earthquake was a huge challenge for ARK.

Elizabeth: So many people lost their homes and couldn't take care of their pets. We took in 600 animals, far more than ever before.

Alice: How did you handle so many animals at once?

Elizabeth: It was really difficult. But a lot of people came to help. Even a group of *bosozoku*, who rode all over, putting up posters saying ARK was taking pets.

Alice: The media coverage after the earthquake brought in a lot of new volunteers. What do they actually do?

Elizabeth: They help with feeding and grooming. They walk the dogs and get them used to being with people, which makes it easier to find them new homes.

Alice: But even if you had thousands of volunteers, that wouldn't be enough if there was another major disaster. Isn't there a long-term solution?

Elizabeth: After Kobe and Tohoku, I now think we need emergency shelters where people can stay with their pets.

Alice: Then people could care for their own pets after a disaster.

Elizabeth: You see? There's always a solution, if you're willing to try something different.

Notes ■ earthquake「地震」 ■ huge「非常に大きな」 ■ challenge「難問、試練」 ■ all over「至る所を」 ■ coverage「報道」
■ bring in「…を連れてくる」 ■ grooming「(動物に)ブラシをかけて手入れをすること」 ■ emergency「緊急」

T O P I C 3 **Don't bite off too much.**

Alice: There are so many animals in need, but you can't help all of them. How do you avoid spreading yourself too thin?

Elizabeth: Well, no one can do everything. If you bite off more than you can chew, you won't accomplish anything. Instead, decide what you can do—what you can actually get done, then do it. Don't start a new project until you have finished what you already started. If you focus, you will achieve.

Notes ■ spread *oneself* too thin「同時に手を広げ過ぎる」(thin は「薄く」という意味)
■ bite off more than one can chew「自分の能力以上のことをやろうとする」(bite off は「食いちぎる」、chew は「かむ」という意味)

Review and Reflect

Congratulations. You've learned a lot in this course about working in Japan. We've heard about many different jobs. Let's review.

We met a sales representative for a publishing company, a tour planner for a major travel agency, a marketing director in charge of five brands of automobiles.

We also met a translator of games and novels, an assistant supervisor at a convenience store chain, the president and CEO of a brewery, and a teacher at an elementary school.

We heard from an architect who designs exciting and interesting buildings, a freelance designer and marketing consultant, a business development manager at a trading company, and the president of an IT recruiting company, the chief technology officer at an IT company, the owner of casual French restaurants, and the chair and founder of an NPO.

Like many of the people we heard from, I'm also a foreigner working in Japan. In my job as a journalist, I interview people every day. But working on this textbook allowed me to talk to people I might not normally meet—people in many different professions, and from many different countries, all of whom have chosen to work in Japan. It was a great opportunity for me to think about why I, too, like working in Japan. I learned a lot—there are so many opportunities to do really interesting work in Japan.

You've learned a lot, too. I'm sure you have been thinking about your own future as we moved through the course. So now, I'd like to ask you some questions:

What sort of work is the best match for you? Why?

What one factor do you think is most important when choosing a job?

What can you do now to prepare for your future career?

I hope you've enjoyed this course, and that it helped you think about your future and what sort of work you'd like to do. I know you've learned a lot of English that will be helpful as you look for a job and enter the working world. There are so many interesting opportunities in Japan—and the world. I'm sure you all have bright, promising futures.

Notes ■ reflect「よく考える、自分と向き合う」 ■ automobile「自動車」 ■ CEO「最高経営責任者」(Chief Executive Office の略)
■ bright「明るい」 ■ promising「有望な」

[撮影協力（ユニット順）]

台東区フィルム・コミッション

明治学院大学

明治学院大学ポール・ハラ准教授

株式会社エイチ・アイ・エス

フィアット クライスラー ジャパン

株式会社ローソン

株式会社協同商事 コエドブルワリー

淑徳小学校

クライン ダイサム アーキテクツ

株式会社グローバルエージェンツ

ワールドネイバーズ護国寺

ACグローバルソリューションズ株式会社

三井物産株式会社

株式会社EPコンサルティングサービス

ル・プティ・トノー

NPO法人アニマルレフュージ関西

[映像制作]

ディレクション……町田賜美
撮影………………有限会社パンアウト
編集………………町田賜美、有限会社パンアウト

教師用音声CD有り（別売） **クラス用DVD有り（非売品）**

Working in Japan [Text Only]
―Video Interviews with 14 Professionals

2015年1月20日　初版発行
2024年1月20日　Text Only版 第2刷

著　者　Alice Gordenker、John Rucynski
発行者　松村達生
発行所　センゲージ ラーニング株式会社
　　　　〒102-0073　東京都千代田区九段北1-11-11　第2フナトビル5階
　　　　電話 03-3511-4392　FAX 03-3511-4391
　　　　e-mail: eltjapan@cengage.com
　　　　copyright©2015 センゲージ ラーニング株式会社

装　丁　　　足立友幸（parastyle）
編集協力　　飯尾緑子（parastyle）
制作協力　　町田賜美
印刷・製本　株式会社平河工業社

ISBN 978-4-86312-409-7